"The globally acclaimed management thinker Dr. Vinayshil Gautam has in this book given us some valuable and thought-provoking essays on a variety of contemporary issues, which are well worth a read."—*Dr. Karan Singh*

■ ■ ■

"Fluidity of human relations calls for flexibility in management systems which seek to maximise capabilities and minimise conflict. 'Echoes' brings us the wit and wisdom of a management Guru, in a rich tapestry of experiences, historical vignettes, literary quotations and, above all, the insights of a sharp intellect tuned to a sensitive soul."—*Dr. K. Srinath Reddy*

■ ■ ■

"The book is very timely and relevant for leaders as they work through their professional careers. It has wide range of topics which Leaders normally go through in their professional careers and will serve as a good guide and help them learn and better understand the situations, equipping them to become better professionals. The real work life experiences have been well illustrated and articulated.

One of the most debated topic in the corporate world is Ethics. Considering the various challenges in the current times, it is imperative to bring this to the fore and ensure that it is properly dealt with.

The book has rightly mentioned—it is all about People Management. A Leader needs to understand their people and have a high level of empathy. This is an important quality which takes centerstage as one goes up the leadership rank.

One of the many lines that I liked is from the chapter Go Home or Go Big—"The thorns of life propel me to move faster and quicker to get beyond the range which takes me to the lush grasses and the beckoning scenario, which unfolds as I keep walking towards the horizon."

This book traverses the journey of a professional and serves as a good guide to help them navigate and has many valuable takeaways."—*Richard Rikhe*

ECHOES

Dr. Vinayshil Gautam

A legend in the world of management thought and practice, Dr. Vinayshil Gautam is internationally acclaimed as an institution builder. As a management expert, he has facilitated Management Development activities in Germany, UAE, Saudi Arabia, Malaysia, and some of the finest organisations in India. His expertise has been sought in some of the key policy formulation activities of the Government and the Corporate sector. He has been on the board of various Indian and non-Indian organisations. He has addressed International audiences from Montreal to Melbourne and Caracas to Tokyo.

He has been a visiting faculty to Institute of Developing Economies, Japan and universities such as Cambridge, Sussex, London, Brunel, UK; Dominican, Duke, Penn State, USA; University of LA, Central University, Venezuela; Toronto, York, Canada, etc.

Widely published, he is a recipient of several fellowships and many recognitions including lifetime achievement awards. Among other things, Dr. Gautam has served as the Founder Director of IIM(K); Leader, Consulting Team, IIM (Shillong); 1st Head Management Department IIT(D), 1st Hony Dean KPMG Academy; Sr. MD and Principle Economic Adviser, Protiviti (I) Member Pvt. Ltd. He has represented India, inter alia, in the activities of UNESCO and Asian Productivity Organisation, Economic Conclave, Morocco. He is President Emeritus of ISTD.

ECHOES

Vinayshil Gautam

CONCEPT PUBLISHING COMPANY PVT. LTD.
NEW DELHI-110059

ISBN: 978-93-88937-00-9

First Published 2021

Published and Printed by

Concept
Since 1974

Concept Publishing Company Pvt. Ltd.
A/15-16, Commercial Block, Mohan Garden,
New Delhi-110059 (INDIA)
T : 91 11 25351460, 91 11 25351794
E : publishing@conceptpub.com *W* : www.conceptpub.com

For

a global leader in Human Resources Studies

Dr. Helmi Sallam

Professor, Cairo University, Cairo

Chairman, TEAM Misr, Egypt

Acknowledgements

This Book stands in the debt of a large number of people, who have helped to initiate, nurture and contribute to a melody of thinking for all that I seek to do. The list is large and cannot be attempted without gaps, which would not be fair to the personal debt I owe to many relationships. They have all helped me to evolve. Hence, the acknowledgement is to all contributors to my growth and learning process.

Without being a reductionist, I would like to name the following people, who contributed in substantial ways to shaping of the deck.

Ayush Gupta is a contender for a special mention. Ayush was in my classes decades ago in IIT Delhi and like many in my classes, he has stayed in touch over the years, and has made a splendid career in the consulting domain, with an outstanding track record. He recalls with nostalgia the details and impact of many sessions and exchanges he had with me, over the years. He believes, it has contributed to clearing his thoughts. He, along with several others, have always felt that, if, I were to be recording some of my experiences in handling life issues, others may also wish to gain from it. The result is in your hands. Ayush did better than just join that group of thought, but also offered to assist in processing the type script of this book. Subsequently, PB Saji from my office, took over.

It is natural for the family members of the author to figure in the acknowledgement of any book. In my case, Shobhana-jee, my wife and our two daughters, Tanvi and Saumya are no exceptions. Shobhana-jee, has not extracted many promises in our marriage, but there is one thing, which she made a clear indent for. Before I stop writing, she wanted me to do what could be considered as the '*magnum opus*' of my writing career. As of today, I have yet to be clear on the shape of that *magnum opus*. But that is another story. So far as this book is concerned, she has had a significant role in the drafting of the texts: being a resident tutor correcting, nurturing and encouraging. Tanvi and Saumya have filled our lives with joy, care and, I might add, learning. That they lead their life in meaningful manner is one of the positive outcomes of the kind of effort this book took.

To my many knowledgeable audiences, editors, readers and critics, grateful thanks for keeping me as a growing person through their involvement, critique and expectations. To the Library staff of many of the repositories I have to be in touch with and the IT professional who keep my referencing system alive, much gratitude.

The Publisher, Nitin Mittal, has been solicitous as always, and this is my sixth title from Concept Publishing Company. He has all the patience to stay with the texts through COVID-19 times and ultimately bring it to light.

Finally, my gratitude to Dr. Karan Singh; Dr. K. Srinath Reddy and Shri Richard Rekhi to encourage me with their comments.

My renewed gratefulness to the numerous unnamed friends and critics: friendly and otherwise. Thank you, dear reader, for making me feel wanted.

Contents

ECHOES: Opening Thoughts

Echoes, as being shared with you, have sixteen rhythms to it. As contained in these pages, it moves through deliberations on topics, such as Success; People; Relationships; Predictive validity; Mythology, Living by one's word; Does the winner take all?; and more.

These are short descriptive reflections arising out of nearly five decades of professional and personal experience. The domain of experience ranges over academia, consulting world, government, corporate life, voluntary societies, private enterprises, domestic environment and a cross section of life experiences sometimes beyond these groups.

Clearly, it (reflection) is imperative in relationships with oneself, between one person and another, between one to a group, between group to a group and group to the larger entities of a community. In each case, one may not necessarily have a one to one relationship; however, community life is a realty in which personal experiences are often embedded.

Each persona lives at various level and each persona is a multi-layered consciousness. A school of thought believes that there are seven different levels of consciousness/experiential realities in every homo-sapien. Be that as it may, understanding of self is a challenge, which even the highly evolved seers have found difficult to grapple with, in its fullness. This effort may not go all the distance, but it is, hopefully, some contribution in the limited domain of 'learning exchanges'.

The expectation is of resonance with the reader. Optimistically, one hopes that reading these pages may also be of some use to the person, beyond just reflection.

Recognizing that no two doors to experiences are ever identical, the texts, therefore, also try to navigate the essentials of learning from each other's experiences. Life would be, entirely, too short, if one was to learn everything at one's own cost.

Over the period of time, these essays evolved; various implications and meaning of the word 'echoes' become clearer. Illustratively, it became more evident that the reputation of an individual/institution/community or whatever else is, also, a matter of 'echoes' of the attributes of the identity of that entity. The attributes of that so called identity may or may not have been tested, but they are a popularly believed to be true. Typically, Germans are believed to be efficient. The Sikhs are often referred to as a 'martial race'. The British are often reputed to be punctual. Examples can be many. These beliefs determine assumptions and often are guide posts to behaviour. These beliefs can be 'echoed' across territories and time. They become potent decision making inputs.

Similarly, the process of branding is a matter of 'echoes' that reverberate about that institution, process or a person. These components are not invariably evidence based. Did not a French thinker say, "Throw enough mud something will stick"?

Folk belief has it that in a US Presidential nominee campaign, several decades ago, a candidate thought of a unique process to create a wave in his favour. Those were the days when the voice amplifier systems were just beginning to get into the market. He fitted the walls of the convention hall with several amplifiers. The amplifiers were, in turn, connected with an announcing system, on tape. When the hall was reasonably full, the announcing device was turned on and the amplifiers began chanting the candidates' name. Coming from the four sides of the convention hall, it appeared as if the crowd was doing the chant and, soon enough, the people in the crowd also took up the chant. The candidate who had organised this appeared to be far ahead of his rival in popular endorsement. He carried the day with ease!

There are other implications of 'echoes'. One must listen to oneself talk to understand how one comes across to other people. Many would not talk the way they do, if only they realized the way they come across to others.

Further, there is the dimension of the 'inner voice'. One must listen to one's 'inner self' if one wishes to be truly fulfilled. Inner satisfaction is the core of personal happiness. The same can be said of 'value systems'. One should be true to one's value system of the positive genre, to be truly achieving, in an enduring manner.

Put simply, among other things, "echoes" are a power instrument of feedback, self-realization and creating a brand. People create their own echoes. Others, also, help create a reputation or a brand for an individual, institution and more by simply echoing an image. Sometimes, it can be controlled or moderated. On many occasions, even making an impact on a popularly echoed belief is a challenge.

'Echoes' have a power which need to grasped, more fully.

The various chapters of the book have been widely shared with a select and discriminating audience and readership in widely different global environments" – from Carcas to Tokyo and Montreal to Melbourne. This has helped to sharpen the insights and the almost global usability of shared experiences that the book seeks to navigate. The attempt is to help without running the risk of being pedantic; learning to share without expecting a compensation.

It is one of the truths of life that if a person 'B' is of support to an individual 'A', that individual 'A' may never come back to help 'B'. However, another individual 'C' may come to help 'B' without having any obligation to do so. Such is the mixed character of interpersonal dynamics that the return need not come from the person one has sought to help.

Yet, all told, somehow, in most of the cases, it works out and the balance sheet need not always be retained for profit and loss.

Ultimately, it is a question of whether it has helped the individual to grow to be a better person and helped groups and more to evolve into a more sensible and empathetic style and content of existence.

Going through the pages would certainly be fruitful for those who care for themselves, like to subscribe to a responsible interpersonal dynamics embedded in a concern for the community at large.

Life is dogged with dilemmas and riddled with paradoxes. Fulfilment comes out of a sense of achievement. There is always a context. If one can progress on a path from 'fluidity of assumptions' to 'action with conviction', incidental experiences can be seen in proportion to the larger meaning and purpose.

Feedback, as always, will be most welcome.

January, 15, 2021 **Vinayshil Gautam**

'Saran'
'O' 27, South City 1
Gurugram, Haryana

Success

What this chapter is, also, about

Success is desired by many, but achieved by few. This chapter helps bring a perspective on the most important, yet overlooked, facets of success. Of particular interest is how success requires a balanced co-existence of internal and external factors, along with a constant frame of reference.

Everyone wants success. Put simply, to a very large extent, success is an act of choice, a frame of mind, and a vantage point of perspective. It's often how one looks at a situation, interprets it, and internalizes it to act on it which will define how successful she/he is.

The proposition is simple: success is an internal feeling of wellbeing, arising out of a conformity to a visualization of a preferred state of being. It is also ensconced in a context of group, communities, and geographical habitats. In all cases, it is a consort of smugness, of achievement, so recognized by the individual and the community to which he affiliates.

Almost everyone has some faith or belief in symbols, and their socialization orient them to read meaning under symbols. For example, many will believe that a black cat crossing the path is a bad omen. There are two ways of responding to it. One is to back away, postpone the movement towards the destination, or perhaps abandon it. The other way of looking at the situation is that nothing is an unmitigated, uninterrupted, smooth flow. If there is an interruption, it is just as well that it happened at the beginning of the act, and go ahead with the confidence of the thought that lightning does not strike twice. The rest will be smooth.

Which of the above two examples appeal to you is a matter of personal choice, orientation, ability to interpret events, and ability to organize one's thoughts and actions. This is only part of the story. There are objective situations, and external factors involved too.

Illustratively, if one doesn't have adequate shelter or enough food to eat, then clearly one is in the grip of poverty, no matter how one defines it. Of the many definitions of poverty, perhaps the simplest one to understand is that poverty is an involuntary deprivation of the basic facilities and amenities of life, as accepted in the community where one is embedded.

Caution needs to be exercised here to avoid confusion. Different communities have different perceptions of amenities and basic needs of life. For some, a common toilet maybe a way of life, and it doesn't occur to them that personalized toilets are achievable. Even if that person sees it as achievable, it may not be an objective in his life to reach that level. A little bit of elaboration of this may help.

One of our relatives of my

grandfather's generation had a floundering campus of a house. If it was outside the city of Allahabad, where this house was, it would have been called a farmhouse. Embedded in the city, in one of the busiest and the most upmarket localities, it could be only a campus of a house. Since it was in India, it wouldn't do to call it a mansion because that's not idiomatic. It would be like explaining the poem of Wordsworth called "Daffodil" to a group of middle school children, who had perhaps never seen anything beyond a rose, a *kena*, a *rajnigandha*, or a *bela* at the best. Notwithstanding the take of the writer, in many textbooks in India, "Daffodil" is still taught to the great misery of the students who cannot visualize it. That's another story.

More to the purpose is the reference to poverty, and what constitutes a bottom line of comfort. Once this is established, the story of success begins to become an escalating story. Like many human emotions, like love, hate, irrationality, success is without boundaries. The more you succeed, the more you desire it. The more you want, the more you work for. Getting there, and once having got there, one needs to learn how, and when to pause, or one starts resetting the goal post.

This is part of the reason why usable texts on success are few. It is the writer's aspiration, that you will be able to select from this stream of consciousness, elaboration of what fits your size.

There are two messages to be given here. One is that success is a personalized experience. Two, success is embedded in a social framework of reference. If success depends on these two aspects, both of them are important to understand.

One is as successful as one believes one to be. As an undergraduate student of a top-grade university in a B grade city, having achieved some prominence with my grades, I was a part of a group playing host to a minister who had flown in to the city on a government aircraft. He was of the same state as where this university was. When we asked him to tell us more about himself, it sounded strange to me, that whereas he was in his mid-50s, he remarked, "What more could I want from life? I have got enough. How much can the son of a peasant get? I am, after all, a peasant's son."

It struck me as odd then, it strikes me as odd now. His framework of reference was a peasant (a *kisan*). He did not specify the amount of land his father had, presumably it was not too much, but if it kept him at a starvation level, that was also not stated. The sense I got was, in his scale of living and occupation, a peasant (*kisan*) is at the bottom of the pyramid. Having become a minister in the central government, he has not only changed professions, but arrived where he believes, and perhaps rightly so, that the society looks up to him. Why the society should look up to a minister is not difficult to guess, especially if the society is resource scarce.

This is not the story the world over. In the Scandinavian countries, it will be difficult to make out on the streets, if somebody was a minister or a mere peasant. In Asia, the writer has visited countries where the minister has walked into the hall, and sat next to him. When the writer introduced himself to the person next to him, he responded with his name, and that he was a minister in the cabinet of that state. This is unthinkable in many other countries, including India.

This brings us to the third dimension, each society has visual

indicators of success. In the olden days, in a function of some consequence, say a marriage or a reception, the number of elephants or horses seen would be counted. Now, the exclusivity of an event is counted by the number of police personnel that are requisitioned, and how much of common movement they block or redirect. Put simply, success comes not only in multiple shapes, but also multiple sizes, multiple colours, and myriad manifestations.

There is no need to feel overwhelmed because any issue is as complex or as simple as one makes it. The writer of these lines, in his mid-50s, took an arbitrary decision after he resigned from being the head of a national institution that he would not look for designations anymore in his career, but focus on cerebral pursuits of reading, writing, speaking, and grooming people to do the same. For livelihood concerns, consult, teach, practice extension education, and did not rule out serving on committees. Life did not bless him with more than a basic house, and a modest vehicle. To this house, at least the writer has never felt to invite the high and mighty just because he did not have a villa comparable to the one which the invitee had. Most have obliged by coming, though a few have always found excuses not to come.

Irrespective, the reference in the preceding para is not to be autobiographical, but to state that success is a frame of mind, and where one choses to freeze the frame.

The story rolls on. That there are social indicators of success has already been referred to above. This is a frame of reference which cannot be wished away. For example, in India, a successful career would mean graduating successively from a village to a *qusba* to a *mufassil* habitat to a town to a city to a metropolis, and thereafter, a global setting, presumably in the chain of New York, London, Tokyo. Families often traverse this route. Some abandon the previous association of the village or the *qusba*. If they keep it at all, it is always as an heirloom, if it can survive sibling animosities and resource crunch. There it is, that the history of urbanization in India is in many ways different from the history of urbanization, say in south of England.

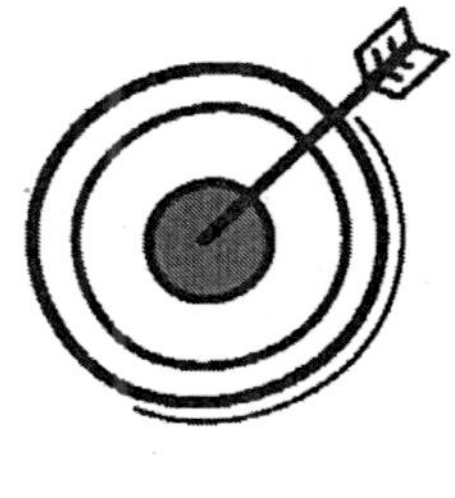

Like all stories, there is more to come

and the missing part of the narration above is that success always requires internal peace and external recognition. Deep within oneself, one may feel to be a success, but if the wife complains of how much more opulent her sister's husband is, and how the husband has still a distance to go to reach his level. Then, somehow personalized descriptions of success tend to give that sense of inadequacy which can only breed discontent. Success can disappear if the frames of reference change.

Besides self-identification, success needs external recognition from the circles which serve as a personal network, a social network, and a professional reference point. Ultimately, it is an act of choice, and the ability to hold one's own living deep inside a babble of contending logic, contending thoughts, and competitive bid situations.

Success would require being alive to one self, and that is as much a matter of personal growth as of external recognition.

All Management Is People Management

What this chapter is, also, about

Most successful professionals spend the maximum proportion of their time in people management. Even the best people managers are loath to hazard a guess as to which techniques work, and which don't. The complexity of the subject, combined with an under-appreciation of its impact, makes this one of the most important topics in the book. The author's expertise and background in organization management brings a unique perspective across domains to the discussion.

There is a well-known Russian story, which may strike a chord with some of the readers, or a feeling of its authenticity regarding solitude. It is about 2 friends — like in many stories — one obscenely rich, and the other, miserably poor. Yet, they were very fond of each other. The bone of contention between them arose one day when the rich friend said that solitude is worse than poverty. The poor friend responded by saying that is because you don't know what poverty is about. You are confusing it with your loneliness of richness — the lack of genuine relationships. Of course, in this conversation between the friends, there was a twist.

Given that both of them were in their mid-20s, presumably with some exposure to gender relationships, personal fondness, and more, to get to the crux of the conversation might be worthwhile. They took a bet between themselves. It went something like this — If the poverty driven friend would remain in the solitude of a room for 25 years; the richly endowed friend would give him 25 billion rubles. There would be a guard outside the room, but the guard would be under instructions not to prevent the inmate to go out of the room. Put simply, the inmate would have the key of the lock, and he could simply unlock himself, and walk out anytime he chose. The guard, however, was to ensure that no one met him, and he talked to no one. This was the rule which would extend through all of 25 years with no exceptions.

The poverty driven friend could order whatever he wanted, eat whatever he wished, dress as he fancied. There was to be only one limitation — no company, no conversation, no communication, simple solitude. The author of the story graphically described what he believed the psychology of this person under self-severance of a lockup for patches of 5 years, 10 years, 15 years, and as the years rolled on. The author goes on to describe how after nearly 15 years, the friend stopped dressing well, and was not very particular about his grooming, and other details which don't fit into this narrative. The climax of the story came a day before 25 years was to be completed.

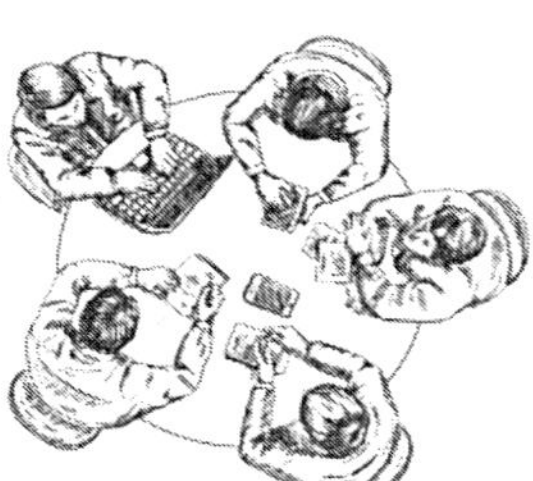

The psychology of the man had undergone such a radical transformation, that he wrote out a long letter to his friend which, put simply, said if I could spend all these 25 years without companionship, what would I now do with the money after I have become unfit for any human companionship? If I couldn't talk when I wanted to, beginning tomorrow, I don't wish to talk when I can. There is nobody I wish to meet, there is nobody I wish to see, no one would remember me anyhow. What would I do with the money? You keep the 25 billion rubles, and give it to any deserving cause you deem fit. So far as I am concerned, this is a final goodbye. Never take this bet with another human being, because if he plays it honestly, he will never find the money worth what it can buy.

The story ends there. The writer of these lines does not know how authentic it would be, because the circumstances of the story are unique, the players are unique and the conclusions certainly marks a simple truth of life. A simple biological truth — humans is gregarious by nature. They need the company of their loved ones. Those who love Urdu poetry would recall a famous couplet where the poet evokes the company of his beloved, so that she may come back and hurt him, only to go away again. (*Ranjish hi sahi, dil hi dukhane ke liye aa*...)

People who lead a life wading through bustling crowds, shouldering their way through uncontrollable throngs in public places, lifts where people see through you, and offices where one picks up the phone to be noticed across transparent glass windows only to be observed whether one is working or talking, will have to stretch their imagination to comprehend that if company can be so overbearing, solitude in its true form can be almost intolerable. The writer does not hope to have every reader agree with this approach. The young ones believe that every emotional bond which they enter afresh will be different to their preceding experiences of heartbreak; while the older ones who

swap jobs hoping that the next boss would be a little more reasonable than the preceding one. There are yet older ones, who are fighting life's blues, while coping with the pangs of growing children who leave the nest, ageing, growing distance in marriage, and stultified careers. Such people desire nothing more than to be left alone.

The typologies can be multiplied, and some readers might identify with some of the mental states outlined above. This comparison and analogy is only as good as far as it goes. The truth, however, is that most organizations find that the main people to contend with are their own people. Most societies have problems of bad traffic, noise at the wrong hours of the day, jostling for spaces on the road, and almost endemic competition for ever receding resources. Amongst the resources, water and air have got included recently. So, the list goes on, and people yearn for solitude.

Like the classical mirage, solitude seems beautiful from a distance, but keeps receding towards the horizon as one approaches it. If there were no people, there would be no society. The writer almost said procreation, but there would be some who wouldn't buy it. In an era of test tube babies, stored ovaries, and frozen semen's where but for the act of life giving combinations, technology has taken over everything. Hence, the tribe of people who believe that people management is an optional extra keeps gathering strength — a palpable fantasy which can only be nailed through abundant experience. Consider two examples — how long one can cry if there was no one to tell you not to do so? Else, how long one could laugh at a joyous occasion, if there was no one else to laugh along with you? Be it sadness, coyness, joy, or whichever form of emotion is being observed and communicated is central to that experience lasting more than

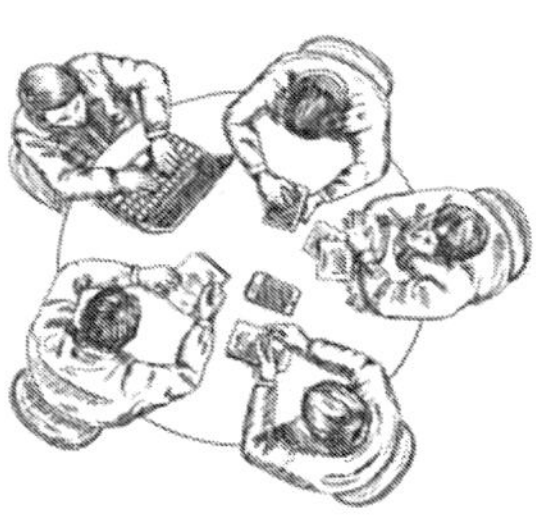

150 seconds. There is nothing sacrosanct about the figure of 150 seconds. It has been deliberately put beyond 2 minutes because of a well-known book, which threatened to create 2-minute managers. Hence, the significance of two minutes in human life.

On an equally serious note, after one has realized the basic truths of human existence, love, anger, agony, triumph, rumination, self-talk, one realizes that to get anything done, one has to deal with people. The writer remembers making a presentation to a group of CEOs on the theory of change, and he began by asking them to ask a question, and one of the corporate czars asked almost sneeringly, “So tell us what is change?” That’s not a question which can be ducked in a public forum. And the writer responded by asking the audience about how many of them were unmarried, and two hands of youngish people went up. So, complimenting them on their state of bliss, the writer quickly went on to mention that for those who were married, the quip would make better sense. Most marriages go through a rumble, if not a tumble (the pun unintended) because when a couple get married, the man goes into the marriage believing that the woman will not change, she does. The woman goes into the marriage with the belief that she will change the man, and she finds that he doesn’t change. Then, the rumble and the tumble begins, and the realities of marriage stare both of them squarely — this time, in their togetherness. That is change.

A peal of muffled laughter swept through the audience, but no one really contradicted. That’s another story. More to the point, it is the unpredictability of people which makes the issue of dealing with people such a fascinating challenge and incapable of being programmed — either in algorithms or even in the current theories of machine learning. People are not just resources, a theory that many computer scientists have warmly

espoused. People are the purpose of action. Hence, there is something palpably amusing about the term human resources department. It would have been perhaps closer to operational efficiency, if it was called job capability department.

The simple truth is no person is hired for a job. It is a person's capability that is hired for the job, which is what makes unlearning, learning, and relearning a matter of such high importance for business success. Technologies are constantly changing because the energy sources are changing. Energy sources are changing because the sources of supply of some of the energy forms is a bounded one. Hence, it is not only human beings who change, but also impact the nature of change. This aspect is usually missed by the best of human resource specialists.

The psychologists come in with their scaling and graphing of attitudes and motivation. The sociologists use their small group dynamics, large group dynamics and neat theories of collective behaviour. The political scientists explain the struggle for the control of the decision making process; but the industrial engineers consider all this so much hot air, because there is no predictive validity with neat categories and extrapolations such as the kind they normally deal with. The disciplines come to naught in dealing with real people. People are essentially similar when it comes to birth, procreation, and death. And yet no two people are alike. The theme is, however, to draw a perspective on how all management is people management and not to lose track of that is important. It becomes people management because machines take on the character of the use patterns of the human hand, and even his touch.

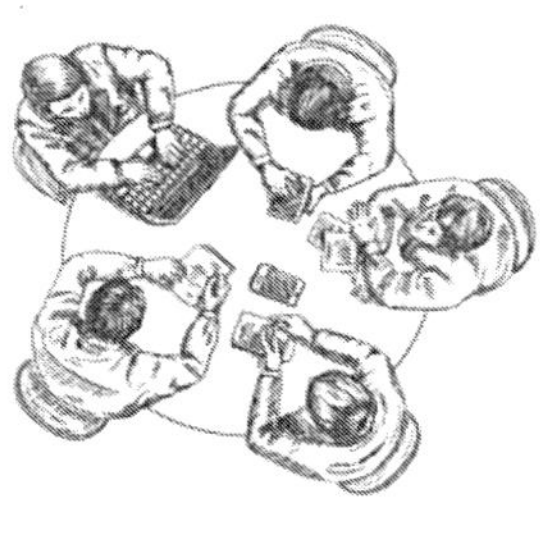

The more perceptive would recall how when cars roll out of an assembly line, all the gear positions are the same. But after some months of usage, no two cars will ever have any of their gears coming at the identical angles that they did when they rolled out of the assembly line. The way the driver settles his first gear, or moves from first gear to second gear, itself impacts the slant of the gear alignment. Hence, in a very real sense, the flow of technology takes on the shape and shadow of human use pattern, be it algorithms of use in artificial intelligence, or the computer driven machines. The nuanced controls affect their operations.

Even machine learning models take decisions for a particular customer facing process. Any person familiar with artificial intelligence and machine learning would recognize that after carefully considering transparency requirements, the better institutions decide to mitigate risks by limiting the types of machine learning algorithms they use. Certain models which are overtly complex and opaque have to be definitely disallowed to strike a balance of comfort. Even though this may be at the cost of certain predictive value, no summa of artificial intelligence will operate the system as if the people factor was simply not in use or of value. It is this ethical aspect which has made the designing of algorithms such a critical part of artificial intelligence algorithms.

If this is the story of people's impact on machine action, then working out the reverse logic of how everything is ultimately about managing people is an exercise in futility. If there were no people, there would be no need to manage. And if there was no need to manage, there would be no need to know if one is mistaken in not going the mathematical route. Therefore, it is proven that all management is rooted in people management.

Relationships

What this chapter is, also, about

An appreciation of relationships, and their power in making or ending a person's growth, is essential for anyone looking to succeed in life, whether personally or professionally. Most people will learn how to form effective relationships by trial and error, typically after a lot of effort and failed attempts. This chapter helps develop an awareness of what drives relationships, as well as their limitations, and is helpful in bringing a frame of reference to the discussion.

Relationships are fundamental to all that exists. It covers the animate and the inanimate.

You might be surprised to read relationships between inanimate objects, but they are for real. Typically, dramatically and perhaps, most inconspicuously, the relationships between planets is central to cosmic existence. One generates heat, the other receives it. If the orbits of the planets were to change, clashes would occur, and the entire solar system could blow up. The believer assumes a cosmic intelligence determining this. The nonbeliever draws comfort by attributing it to nature, whatever that means. Relationships help to establish classifications, such as similar types of rocks, and practicing reverse engineering, trying to establish how they could have originated, and thereby reading meaning to what appears inconsequential, or not so inconsequential situations.

Inanimate material such as oil, coal, and other fuels keep the planet going. Indeed, some of the most valued objects of the animate world and existence come from inanimate sources such as diamond, gold, platinum, and so on. Enough has been said in the preceding lines to make a simple point of relationships and inanimate existences. The glitch is that somehow talking of relationships has been confined to the animate world, and even there, to human beings.

This is a palpably incomplete universe of conceptualization, and has its own inherent pitfalls. Other than human beings, there are intelligent existences on this planet in many forms. There are plants which are intelligent in more senses than one, and as a good botanist will tell you, there is no such thing as an unintelligent plant. The list can cover creepers, flowers, trees, and rivers. The animals have their own intelligence, and the much mooted intelligence of the dolphins or the dogs is only one aspect of the intelligence of the animal kingdom. Hence the propensity of homo sapiens to attribute intelligence, and therefore, relationships to its own existence is not necessarily a proven dogma. One consequence of intelligence, by definition, should be recognition of a relationship and being conscious of inter-dependencies. In many ways, specie for specie, animals are smarter than the humans. Illustratively, no animal eats its own. The chequered history of homo sapiens is too well known to the knowledgeable, perhaps too gory, to need elaboration. To put it simply, relationships when they develop an equilibrium,

help achieve a gradient of comfort, if not an elevating plateau of relationships.

This interdependence of people and things is recognized in the Indian idiom, but is often written off by those who learned to interpret relationships and events in the Anglo-Saxon or transatlantic perspective. This Hindu view nevertheless survives because of its inherent strength. Existence of this planet is possible only by recognition and nurturing of relationships between the intelligent "homo sapiens" and the plants and the animal kingdom. When so-called development perspectives have rapaciously poached on this equilibrium, repercussions on climate, ecology, and the very heart of human existence indeed, are more than likely to be disastrous. The results are there for all to see. For the sake of the future of this planet, one hopes good sense will prevail in stabilizing the equilibrium of different types of existence of this planet.

Even a cursory introduction to Sanskrit literature indicates that the jungle was not a wild place. It was a place where intelligent life mutually co-existed. It helped the recluse to get away from the hustle bustle of market places, political capitals, army camps, and cities to a life of reclusive, peaceful, and constructive existence. The concept of ashram was not one of conspicuous consumption, or display of artificial luxuries sustained by continuously stoking the embers of mistaken innovation, but in a rhythmic unison of what alone would stand the test of time. The strange thing about nature is that, by its very character, it is unforgiving. It does not respond to petitions of mercy or indeed tearful regrets of recognition of an error. It relentlessly upholds natural justice (the pun on that phrase is totally unintended).

For those who are wondering what this reference is about, the explanation is simple. If somebody does violence to what his system can absorb through eating volumes unthinkingly, or drinking in excessive measure; not only does the belly and the digestive system practice retribution, but very often the nervous system and the judgmental process can get affected. The record of homo sapiens learning from somebody else's experience, is at the best, poor. There is a glib feeling, especially amongst the smart thinkers, that their bodies can take the punishment/ they can get away with it/ they will not be affected by it. Worst of all, they ask how does it matter? A possible response to this kind of extravagant belief in the supremacy of human intelligence is to let such a person think so. Allow such a person to experience nature's retribution, and hope that greater wisdom may have dawned at the end of it. One of those regrettable, but inevitable truths of life is that very often it doesn't, even at the end of the tunnel.

Coming closer to the expectations and the anticipations which the topic of relationships evokes, it may be well worth to remember that the foundation of all relationships is a relationship with oneself. In management circles, it is often peddled as approaches to self-management. It sells well, it makes careers, sometimes it produces results, but invariably it gets attention. Revenues, of course, follow. So, the theme of management itself has progressively acquired a cult status.

It's another matter, that there is very little new to say in it. Most of the world's thinkers, from Confucius and Jesus Christ to Krishna to Schopenhauer to Ruskin, and others have exhorted us to know ourselves, before you can venture to understand others. said similar things like Christ saying, "How is it that you can see the speck in your brother's eye, and not the beam in your own?" This has been repeated over and over again everywhere. The ancients in India began life by saying *"Atmanam viddhi"*, that is know yourself. The truth is that in dyadic and group conversations, a favourite punchline is, "Then you don't know me". It's little use telling anyone why anyone should bother with knowing

anyone else, when people don't know about themselves. It's another matter that everyone believes he knows himself.

Enough has been written, stated, and peddled on this topic, from metaphysics to interpersonal dynamics to make it unnecessary to attempt to sum up, or make an effort to add. How much of it is usable has never been assessed. Hence, as always, assessment is a luxury of those who would have pretensions of being scientific, or helpless that the way forward can only take place through evaluation. There is nothing wrong with that. The missing link is the argument that assessment is fine as long as it is done with recognition that it can be never be terminal. If the framework of reference changes, and standards of acceptability change; then assessments can and do fluctuate. Hence a simple proposition. To deny the value of assessment is foolish. To swear by its infallibility is stupid. The difference between foolishness and stupidity is the difference between not being able to do something because one doesn't know, and doing something with the smugness of being right. The difference is so large that it runs the danger of being written off as excessive conceptualization.

There are three weapons of disrupting progress. They are ridicule, ignoring the value of a contribution, and above all, claiming it's abstruse. Singly or together, they are the most potent weapons to kill an idea. Usually, it is handy with the people who have political or social influence, or the gift of the gab to hold anyone who would not fall in place, and treat them as an avoidable plague. To get back to the proposition of a scientific approach to relationships between one person and another, object, or non-living thing is more to the point of this text. It's important to realize

that to try to connect is a basic human urge. People can connect, obviously to another of their species, nature, and environment. Equally important, it is important to be connected to inanimate objects also. If the last were not true, no family heirlooms would exist, and no one would wear a wedding ring. Human propensity to connect is fundamental, and evokes a lot of emotion, one almost said endocrinal secretion to sound scientific. It's not the intention of these lines to deride scientific approach because it helps to give an important perspective to a scientific problem. However, scientific approach by itself cannot be a panacea to all complex problems — that's another matter altogether.

Recently, a study has been reported from the University of Versailles, Saint-Quentin-En-Yvelines (France) which claims living alone is positively associated with common mental disorders in the general population in England. This was published in the journal *PLOS ONE*. The researchers used data on 20,500 individuals aged 16-24 living in England, who participated in the 1993, 2000, and 2007 National Psychiatric Morbidity Surveys. A questionnaire was used, focusing on neurotic symptoms. The details of the research study don't fit into this narrative. The conclusion maybe worth referring to. The positive association between loneliness and mental disorders has already been referred to. In different subgroups, living alone increased a person's risk for common mental disorders by 1.39 to 2.43 times.

Today, like in many areas, there are buzzwords even in this. It's called simple depression. Of course, if the habit is to build castles in the air, somebody collect, the rent. Usually, he is called a psychiatrist. The complexities of relationships are so large that they are fundamental to all living beings. Yet, the reader of these lines might be conditioned to expect some takeaways, and it would be a legitimate expectation. The enumerations above would not necessarily be of interest to all who would seek guideposts to simple aspirational issues of relationships, or balms to relationships that were valuable, but have got ruptured. People want relationships with their superiors, at peer level, and with their

dependents, even if they are subordinates at the workplace.

There is a simple rule of thumb which governs all this. That is, people relate to others, either as an element of satisfaction, or as an element of future expectations. In either case, the spirit of aspiration is the theme.

Besides the casual relationship forged while travelling or cocktailing (a word coined for the occasion), or simply finding oneself next to another, one starts talking because one believes one has something to say, or would want something to hear; even if it be something else, not leave the mind idle. Hence, relationships can be at many levels, ephemeral, casual, having a short life cycle — attractive, gripping, and fundamental to one's existence. The categories are by no means exhaustive. What is to be understood is, mistaking the quality of one relationship for another can often be a source of grief.

Especially, in dyadic relationships, matters can, and do go wrong, if both the parties don't have at least 51% of overlap in their expectations of each other or aspirations. For a relationship to be stable, the parties have to go grow together at a relatively compatible pace. By the same token, if something most fulfilling crosses the path of one party, the second one can feel betrayed. The important thing to remember is that all relationships can, and do come to an end. The good Hindu will tell you of relationships transcending lives and souls in communion. The writer has no claims to insights or expertise in relationships across different incarnations.

Limiting oneself to the mundane concerns of the superior, the peer level, and the subordinate relationships, one has to recognize

that the other party can, and does move along. This happens between parents and children. It happens in work situations, it happens in casual flings, the ability to let go and recognize the identity of the other person gracefully and willingly is the key to one's own happiness. If the other person has to move on, he or she will. Making it more difficult and complicated and overlaying it with loyalties, penalties, parental claims, and sibling demands is like stretching the elastic band. It will happen for a while, it will happen to an extent, but either it will hit back or break. It is difficult to be conclusive on the theme of relationship, but one wisdom which is as old as the rivers, is captured in many expressions of classical languages. In Sanskrit, it is "*Sansariti iti samsara*" that which moves makes the world. In Latin, it is "pantherae" or everything changes. Surely, there are similar quotations in Greek, Tamil, Chinese, and other languages.

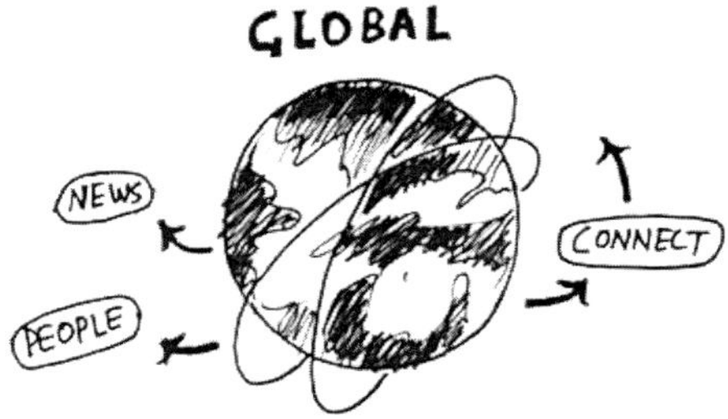

Sounds, Words, and Vocabulary

What this chapter is, also, about

Many amongst you may have wondered that why is it that the most successful people from across diverse walks of life use a vocabulary different from everyone else? Experts tell us that the average English speaking adult has a vocabulary of ~20,000 words. The critical role that a large repertoire of words plays in effective communication is a point very well illustrated by the author's experiences and stories in this chapter.

The Indian school of thought believes that creation began with the resonance of the word *Om*. It was then translated verbally into *shabadam braham mayam jagat.* The world is the resonance of the word. Many refer in everyday communication to the word as *shabad* (word). *Shabad* is literally the sound. To elaborate on this theme would run the risk of sounding abstruse. The average human mind abhors complexity. For the purposes of communication of this particular section, it is enough to say that the transmutation of sound through the grace of cosmic energy acquired material form. Hence, the importance of sound in everyday living, in every form of creation and complexity. All communication is communication of ideas and experiences. Hence, the significance of the "word". Word is a symbol of sounds. The human brain associates certain sounds with certain imagery. When the ear receives certain sound waves, certain imagery is evoked in a part of the brain, and the human mind understands. This is the worth of a vocabulary. However, the truth of life is words mean different things to different people. Words have a cultural connotation. We live in an era where legislatures in any state of India, show their displeasure and derision with chanting of the word "Shame, shame". When shamed, the person so accused is to bury himself in ignominy and disrepute, if not inflicting on himself a worse fate.

Switch scenes to south of England. Somebody misses a bus, and is late at a meeting at work by 10 minutes. He enters the meeting, and half abashedly says, "Mr. Chairman, I'm sorry. I missed my bus". The chairman is very likely to respond, "What a shame, please sit down". Clearly the meaning of the second shame is of a different texture, shade, and connotation than the first shame. Many languages are spoken in so many geographically dispersed segments of their users that it's almost difficult to say if Indian English is comprehensible to a person who has grown up on Scottish English. Any number of Indians wanting to congratulate someone over something would say, let me go and thank him. Now where in the world would a dictionary say that thanking a person means congratulating him? But an Indian to another Indian is perfectly comfortable in this usage.

Examples of this can multiply in every language. This includes Indian languages, Slavonic languages, and as indicated, any language which is spread over disparate territories. Hence, the meaning of the word lies in its usage. The complexity doesn't end there. There is the business of accent. It is an exercise in bewilderment to have one person talk in Australian English, and another in American English. Their accents change the rhythm of words in a manner which best of the linguists find a challenge to unravel in a reference book. Therefore, the only rule which would apply to the situation of communication is — if you can convey what you mean to the person at whom you are beaming the message, it's successful communication. If one believes the narration of complexities, and the slippery character of words or vocabulary is now fully explored, there is more to come.

There is a vocabulary of class. There is also the vocabulary of thinking in one language, and speaking in another language. Consider the English sentence, "I want that only" or "I only want that" or "Only I want that". The change of the location of the word "only" alters the meaning totally. If the Indian is from a particular part of the country where he is translating his thoughts in Punjabi to English as a spoken language to a person who understands only Australian English, it can lead to a not so funny situation.

The writer remembers a story of an Australian who knocked at the doors of a gentleman in Allahabad at 9 o'clock at night with a reference from a friend in Melbourne of the gentleman from Allahabad. When the person opened the door, the person from Allahabad looked at him with a questioning look on his face. The Australian said, "I am so and so and I came to die". He meant, "I am so and so, and I came today". His host practically closed the door on his face, and said, "Not here. Please go somewhere else to die". It appears funny on narration; it wasn't on the evening when this happened because the Australian had nowhere else to go to that evening. He had to keep knocking on the door to say that I have a letter from so and so introducing me as his host took some time to open the door again and receive the letter.

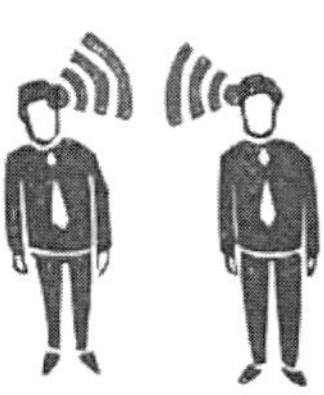

Hence, words not only mean different things

to different people, but pronunciation, like accent can do wonders in either sense to the spectrum of communication. Effective communication, therefore, cannot be taught. It can only be learnt. The trouble with learning anything at any point of time, and in any domain, is only a factor of perceiving the need to learn. Somebody who makes a living out of arranging conferences once told the writer, it is so much easier to get speakers for a conference than to get registered participants for a conference. Everyone wants to talk, very few want to listen, and those who come to listen, have usually both their eyes riveted on who can they connect with to their advantage in the hall, and better still, is the cuisine really worth the cost that has been charged for participation? Listening and learning is a nice hook to weave the activity on. However, the reality is often what is stated above.

Hence, communication is an art of default. Consider the pious statements of all the great spiritual leaders of the world, of which such a large number have been born in Asia. The gist of the teaching can be summed up almost on the back of a postage stamp. Be honest, practice integrity, don't do to others what you don't want others to do to you. Notwithstanding that, the 10,000 years of recorded history of this planet shows that these people were succeeded repeatedly by others, who repeated their message. Their repetition goes on today expanding in numbers, creating new art forms, and almost converting itself to the status of an industry. The only profession which brings in the goodies more lavishly than politics is preaching simplicity and honesty. Most places of worship are surfeit with people who want to ensure that their ledger is maintained in the right manner somewhere upstairs. Therefore, there is no shortage of donations, gifts, and offerings.

Notwithstanding anything which is said above, and certainly no disrespect or irreverence is intended, the fact of the matter is effective communication is conspicuous by its absence.

From this, larger issues of planetary evolution, and inter-professional comparative earnings, one could reduce it to dyadic conversations. The biggest stumbling block between two intended lovers is the statement, "But you have not understood me". Both sides are pleading for understanding, and never receiving it in sufficient manner at the correct time. No wonder heartbreaks are now as common as the crumbling of ceramics.

This notwithstanding, no one has actually given up falling in love. Each time one is given the shove, one lands back in the same domain, hoping that this time communications will be better. They seldom are because values differ, vocabularies differ, assumptions differ, socialization background differs, education differs, and attitude to wealth and work differs. What is constant is visual attraction, and certain commonality of feeling when flesh meets flesh. That is very natural, but never goes far enough to complete a relationship. Communication remains the core of the bond, but is missing.

The poets have sought to sort out this problem by talking of communication between the eyes, communication of touch, and people have even talked of communication of silence. The writer remembers an adage, "If you don't understand my silence, you won't understand my words". An impressive quote, it has been used with devastating effect by many to many, but still it doesn't solve the mystery of communication.

One is entitled to ask like an engineer, "What is the grammar of silence?" To which the reply would be, "That, my dear, is poetry". To which the repartee is, "put it in words"; leading to the answer, "My poetry is the poetry of silence". And before someone starts pulling his hair out, the writer hopes that a simple point has been made: communication is also all about what cannot be defined.

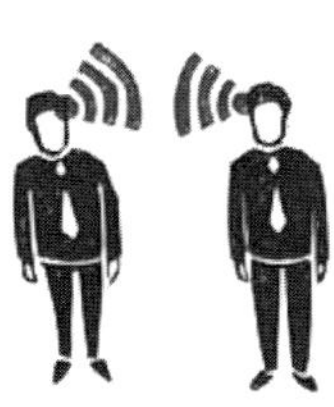

To leave the narrative at this stage would be heresy, because families cannot run on silence, organizations even less so. And nations survive on talking shops, which are sometimes called legislative assembly, or at other times, senate, and still others, parliament. Add to the list, cabinet and if nothing more, advisors to the head of the country. Everyone is supposed to talk. Ultimately, the algorithm of talk is determined by the kingpin of the situation. What he understands is good communication. What he does not understand is abstruse. So, to get to the operational part of sound, words, vocabulary, and communication is essentially a rhythmic phenomenon, where two people or more can move in tandem. It comes only through experience and conscious effort.

A simple belief is that we have to work together and hence, we have to understand each other. This means we have to talk to each other. And you must make an effort to be understood as to what is on your mind to make sure you give the same privileges to the others. This requires huge patience because notwithstanding the brilliant writings of Marks and Engels, Kant before them, and Lenin after them, human beings are not essentially equals. Even today, they deliberate passionately whether it is important to weigh the eggs or to count them.

One does not seek to enter this debate, but the truth is one should at least agree to disagree intelligently. For this, active listening is a must. It is progressively becoming like the art of calligraphy, much admired but used only in exceptional situations of outbursts of emotion or display of class.

The superior demands dominance in a conversation by expecting his selection of words, emphasis, pauses to be reflected by the subordinate, to be able to have a relationship with him. At a peer level, the expectation is that if you love me, think like me. And if you don't think like me, I reserve the right to veto. Then, the non-verbal communication steps in, and of course, physical violence is not necessarily ruled out. There are fond notions of the stronger gender and the weaker gender. Experience has shown that this is a myth. The

weaker gender is essentially the stronger gender. For this, you need only get the testimony of any member of the so called stronger member on what it is to face the wrath of a person of the weaker gender. Even Shakespeare had said, "Hell hath no fury stronger than that of a woman scorned". Being gentle is a nice thing, and so is dressing well and posturing. Stylized communication always makes an impact. Whether it can be enduring or not, or the basis of a relationship which is supposed to be beyond an evening, is a question that need not be discussed here.

Be it sound, words, or vocabulary, the more successful person has always a range at his command. Whether a person can speak many languages or not is a moot point. But he must have mastery over many class of vocabularies, may class of communications and many class of practice of pauses in a conversation to get the right results at the right time, in the right place. And that is the simple craft of communication, on which a whole industry stands ranging from effective inter-personal communication to effective public speaking. So called experts have produced cans of packaged solutions, well packaged, well projected, well branded. This itself is a source of revenue, the likes of which are few in the learning domain.

Opportunities

What this chapter is, also, about

Opportunity is a function of frame of reference and prioritization, rather than an objective concept. Many people believe that they don't get opportunities, or that they are not lucky. This chapter helps bring a perspective to this discussion, and identify the role played by opportunities in success.

There is a phrase in many circles, but more so in that of negotiations — "Frame of reference". It is an attempt to put meaning into apparent randomness. One puts together what one understands, and eliminates what doesn't make sense to the person, or is apriori abhorrent. The truth is, abhorrence is difficult to define because revulsion is a factor of many elements, not the least of which is conditioning. Conditioning is a factor of prenatal experiences, early childhood experiences, and of course, socialization. It touches all sorts of situations, with rituals of purity, pollution to vegetarianism to non-vegetarianism and sub classes of vegetarianism and non-vegetarianism: words, assumptions on the opposite gender, assumptions on wealth, the dos and don'ts of life, and the list can be multiplied manifold. To get back to the frames of reference, negotiation is possible only with minimal acceptable degree of overlap in the frameworks of reference. Otherwise, negotiations degenerate into a very simple principle, "I will keep what I have, and share what you have". Clearly, this cannot be the algorithm of a solution. That people persist in it is only because they believe they are smarter than the other person. Ultimately, like so many other things, it becomes a mind game. The trouble with the rules of the mind game is, everyone considers himself smarter than perhaps anyone else in the world, and certainly, the person he is dealing with. This is not a glib generalization. However, the writer is unlikely to get away with this, unless he provides some evidence. The evidence is in the next paragraph.

I have yet to meet a person who doesn't lie. The extent, the reach, and the spread of falsehood is of course a factor of personality. But everyone does lie. All falsehood and lying is rooted in the belief that the person doing so will get away with it. Hence, it confirms the assumption that everyone believes he is smarter than the others. But the contradictions don't end there. Lying maybe socially disapproved, but being truthful doesn't get universal acclaim either. The usual response to a person who is simple, straightforward, honest is, "Surely, honesty is a good thing, but not to this extent". In fact, a tempered pursuit of truth is the foundation of a good relationship. Inevitably, the issue of proportion comes in, and being truthful does not get pride of place in the pantheon of desirable social qualities for which people would like to train themselves. Hence, human existence in the domain of the mind game becomes not just problematic, but a riddle wrapped in an inscrutable enigma. People have to find their way through it.

The narrative must stop here, in terms of its exploration of falsehood, truth, relationships, and more because this section is supposed to talk of opportunity. Whereas, what is said above may be of some interest to many, the question would inevitably be framed: "What has all this to do with opportunity?" The answer is simpler than can be imagined. Opportunity is a mind game. It is a matter of definition. That external indicators have been attached to it is an attempt to simplify its grasp, and multiply the peddling of one's own ideas.

Everything is an opportunity, depending upon one's vantage point of perception. For a disadvantaged family to grow in social and economic stature is an opportunity, because the baseline for improvement is so low. Being born in a prosperous family is an opportunity, because all the elements for success are setup already, including the launchpad. All statuses between the two polarities are also opportunities. It's just a question of how one looks at it. Hence, opportunity becomes an undifferentiated concept. You have as much opportunity as your palm is capable of grasping, and your mind is capable of operating.

A collateral question then arises, how come then some achieve success, and other "fail"? This is also not a complex question to answer, because the vantage point of perception opens the door of opportunity, but the ability to develop one's potential and gather the resources defines it.

Narratives of successful people are dotted with anecdotes of tenacity, perseverance, and ability to move on with the times. This atomization of success is very often posthumous, because it rationalizes what is already acknowledged. If the same person with the same effort does not achieve success, then, the same tenacity will be described as bullheadedness; perseverance will be substituted with inability to read the writing on the wall; ability to move on with the times would be substituted by running ahead of times. It's a

play on words, enriched by hindsight, garnished by apparent insight, and peddled with aplomb.

The writer would not like to be judgmental about this, because it is the livelihood of many commentators. That is not the problem. The problem is the commentaries create models of success or failure without the audience realizing that much of it is wisdom acquired in hindsight.

Hence, this text is at a very simple point. See opportunity as a no-choice situation. See opportunity as a vote for continuing to live. See opportunity as a way of developing oneself, and achieving what one finds fulfilling. It is a personalized description, pursuit of activities with such a framework of opportunity makes life roll out without regret. It's not difficult to realize that there is no question of 100% success in all one's pursuits.

Hence, pursuit of an opportunity has to be tinged with a sense of realism. The *Bhagwat Gita* has some views on this. It essentially sums up success as being a factor of time, skills, technology, place, and a measure of luck. It is this factor of luck which cannot be programmed, or put into an algorithm. Even artificial intelligence has not graduated to that level yet.

It may be disappointing news to the people with full faith at the altar of artificial intelligence, but it can be claimed that that stage of infallibility of artificial intelligence is not even on the horizon as of now.

Therefore, opportunities are universal. They need to be pursued with a sense of realism. Different professions have viewed this differently. The poet says, "I fall upon the thorns of life and I bleed". The mountaineer says, "I must put my foot on Mount Everest, for no better reason than that Mount Everest is there". There is perhaps little in common between the two statements other than vantage point of perception, and one might add, interpretation.

All human beings are the same, because their

limbs are similar, their inner organs are similar, they are all driven by similar emotions of love, hate, anger, and more. What varies is the shape, the size, the coming together of all this in a unique manner which defines the personality of a human being. Also, no two human beings are the same. So too for opportunity.

There is an opportunity for everyone all the time. It is a question of having a frame of reference, and having a sense of judgement. Insight always helps. However, there is an operational side of opportunity. One may have a platform, and the best of accompanists, but one must have the voice of a singer and the skill to render a melodious song. The natural qualities of a singer would be nature's gift, but the ability to use it is by man's dint of effort. Hence, it is back to combination, permutations, and mixing together of elements which are at times in common but in totality are also unique.

In everyday parlance, talking of opportunity has become the antidote to the depression of failure. It is commonplace to define failure as an opportunity. Maybe it is. More, maybe it should be because it reduces the pain of failure, and strengthens the will to move on. This text, while meant for a certain state of predisposition lays no claims to being exhaustive in its exploration of all the potential. Put simply, everything is an opportunity. It is that trigger which initiates action. It is that therapy which cures pain, and it is that energy which propels more coherent action.

However, as indicated earlier, it does not move on its own. It has to be developed, chiseled, shaped, and propelled to get going. That is what learning, training, and skill formation is all about.

All these things end up in the crucible of lifelong learning and self-development. Going to school, a decision that more often than not is taken by others than the individual affected, going to college, sometimes a shared decision, sometimes not so much, but subsequently in the adult stage, personal decisions become the bedrock of gearing up for opportunity. Any narrative like this, personalized

as it is, would raise the issue of companionship, sometimes refer to as spouse. This dyad may not be a focus of this text, but put simply, it's easier to pursue an opportunity with a cheerleader next to you, and who has faith in you.

Essentially, gregarious as human beings are in nature, we all need company, we all enjoy company, and we are all motivated by company. To be positioned for opportunity, it is important to choose well, not necessarily the best accomplished because that's usually an idea which can be tossed around. It is useful to choose somebody who genuinely believes in your uniqueness, and is likely to live it with conviction. It is one of the many tragedies of life that, the skillful use this at a stage of life to gain a relationship when they want, and dilute it when the relationship goes stale. That is another story.

Opportunity is what we are talking about here, and opportunity requires being proactive. It is like a bald headed creation which has a tuft of hair only in the forefront. If you want to hold that head, you have to hold it from the front. If that has slipped your grasp, your hand will slide over the pate. Hence, opportunity also requires foresight. Foresight requires extrapolation. Extrapolation is based on information and experience, and that doesn't come without combining perspiration with inspiration.

All opportunities don't appear to everyone. Having an eye for opportunity is being a gifted person, and it helps one to get a headstart, beat competition, not by chasing others out, but by simply being ahead. This quality is not only needed in the pursuit of opportunity, but also in interpersonal dialogue and negotiations, besides in much else.

Opportunity is what life is all about, and to live it is to live life.

Predictive Validity

What this chapter is, also, about

The desire for predictive validity has tripped many decisions, and by extension, many rising careers. This chapter talks about the fine balance between uncertainty and predictive validity, along with how to deal with both with equal comfort. Many situations that seem predictable and repeatable are also, in fact, subject to chance and vagaries of time/ nature. Learning to manage uncertainty is a key tenet of an all rounded individual. This chapter is a good starting point to build this skill.

There is a story of a film being shot where the hero was to pick a fight with someone impromptu, make it as physical as possible, and before he could be hit back, the director would intervene. The shot would be okayed, and the victim would be informed that it was just for the shooting of a film. This approach became necessary because several dramatized and simulated situations of conflict hadn't appeared real enough for canning the reel, or making it a part of the movie. Hence, the best option was to make it live, impromptu, but keep it under control. That would really liven up the film. It was, therefore, decided that the hero would walk down the corridors of a marketplace, pick up a quarrel with somebody coming from the opposite side, be really rude to him till it nearly came to fisticuffs. Before it really escalated, the director would intervene. To keep it as real as possible, the lead character of the film was allowed to choose the subject of altercation, and choose his words. Obviously, there were not going to be too many.

The entire crew and the cast felt very happy with this so called innovation to make the altercation as live as possible, to make the film even more real. So, the cameras were set, and the hero started walking down the corridor. As chance would have it, the first person who he saw coming from the opposite side was accompanied by a pretty lady. The hero accosted the man and said, "Excuse me sir. And who may this pretty lady be?" The man was taken aback, and predictably asked, "And what is that to you?" So, the hero said, "Excuse me sir, but as you walk down the corridor, I took it that you were man and wife, the way you were walking down, and I couldn't help wondering, how a distinguished and successful looking person like you could be married to such a decrepit woman?" At the end of the sentence, the hero took a calculated step back, put up both his forearms, and was expecting an assault. Instead of the assault, the man turned around to the lady, and said to her, "You see darling. Now, even the people on the streets are asking the same question which I have always asked you." Obviously, the shot was ruined because there was no assault. Therefore, no fisticuffs, and the whole episode had taken a direction which would be totally unexpected by the author and the director.

So much for predictive validity. It makes a very simple point, people react differently to the same statement, because they get provoked differently. The reaction is internal to them, and not determined by an exogenous factor.

Notwithstanding this all too common an approach to behavioral unpredictability, predictive validity is an eternal quest.

Not only is predictive validity an eternal quest, but so is the urge to know the future. If nature abhors a vacuum, the human mind always looks for certainty, and clarity about the destination, even if it be unfavorable. This is understandable, and predictable. The trouble in arriving at the conclusion is the crux of the matter.

Different authors have used different terminologies for it, and the common expression is, "the contingent and the unforeseen." All these phrases, the hinge factor, the contingent, and the unforeseen, point to a simple truth of the situation. All the elements in their fullness are never known, and hence, can never be accounted for. Forget battles, empires have been lost by some unforeseen or contingent factor determining the day. The way to negotiate it cannot be to ask for more specificity and greater clarity. There are clearly limits to that. What happens is that approximation does not work well enough to give certainty. Yet, approximation remains the best achievable option.

There is no such thing as 100% certainty in any prediction. Anyone in insurance business will tell you that there can be no such thing as 100% guarantee. But, that does not take away from the charm of the approach of predictive validity.

To understand predictive validity, one has to replicate a situation in its entirety to be certain that if these factors, this measure are in play, then this will happen. The truth of the matter is, the factors change, their quality changes. No two contexts are the same, and never do all the players approach the same situation from the same vantage point, or with the same vision. Hence, the fundamental law of predictive validity can only be, if all the factors are known, all the factors are the same, and the context is the same; then the results will be the same.

In recognition of this, the best of engineering sciences have talked of prediction with a certain level of confidence. Say in flood control measures, the water resources engineer will tell you, the planner, that if so much is invested on the banks; if the river flow has this speed and volume; and if so much is invested in this particular type of dam; the prediction of controlling the water flow will have, say, 92% confidence of coming true. He will also advise the planner that if you want to raise the level of confidence of the prediction, then you have to raise the level of investment in the precautionary and the controlling measures. Stretch this logic as you will, no water resources engineer will ever predict with a guarantee of a 100%.

Be it behavioral sciences, or be it engineering sciences, and all that comes in between, predictive validity is one of those eternal quests which is nice and necessary to keep in mind; but which can go only so far. However, certainty is fundamental to comfort. Marriage is a great institutional example of this kind of certainty. The difference between a live-in relationship and marriage is essentially this. A live-in relationship can be broken at will anytime. A marriage has witnesses, a sanctity, social norms, and above all, the approval or disapproval of the context and the community. It is quite another matter that the context and the community can itself become oppressive, and marriage itself, in some cases, become a pain. That is another story.

The purpose of this text is not to discuss the shades of marriage. The purpose of reference to marriage is to identify the driving force of predictability and stability which put a man and a woman together. You grant and accept certain claims and

obligations for a lifetime. And even though divorces are known to happen, can happen, and in certain cases, if one might be forgiven for saying so, become necessary; the ultimate goal of marriage remains a lifelong relationship. This then creates a home, and marriage is the bedrock of a home. One comes back at a point of time to one's choice, need, whatever else to enter a familiar environment where one can have one's way to one's satisfaction. All of it being shared and something to which all contribute. The home then becomes a place for love, enjoyment, recuperation, and revitalization. These elements can be added to.

The burden of the analysis is predictive validity. The first few paragraphs were devoted to point out how definitionally prediction is a risky proposition. It then did touch upon how that risk can be mitigated, and as full explorations would have it, the immediate preceding paragraphs show how the quest for predictive validity is the driving force for human existence. There are other forces for predictive validity. In research particularly, where it is the research methodology which is screened, rather than the conclusions reached, the eternal question remains: what is the predictive validity of this method? If we follow it, where does it take us?

Interestingly, the scientific method has as many votaries in the quest of certainty because they believe that science by nature is predictable, it can be programmed, and there is always a pattern. That debate cannot be resolved in these pages. However, an interesting analogy becomes relevant. All the saints and the seers, the philosophers and the prophets, plough the same furrow conceptually and in ideas. They talk of human nature with its predictability, and literature is not far behind. In Shakespeare's *Merchant of Venice*, Shylock putting his classical defense of the Jews by suggesting something like, "If you hit us, are we not hurt? Are we not in pain?" In other words, all human beings are the same. They all suffer pain when they are hit, they all feel sad when emotionally they lose someone. Operationally, they don't achieve what they set out to achieve. They all feel happy when they get what they want, and they all feel that working better will produce better results.

Yes, be it philosophy, or literature, the idea of predictive validity is as common as it is in the domain of the sciences and engineering. It is one of those strange ideas of human existence which is like a foundation or a cornerstone of much human action, and much human endeavor. It not only gives comfort, but whets our appetite. The quest for certainty and dependability remains eternal in human breast. And yet, the protagonists of creative thinking, and innovative action will argue that learning to live with ambiguity and grey areas is the mother of all fresh thinking. Certainty creates the divide between the dark and the bright, between the right and the wrong. Yet, human life is a testimony to huge areas of grey where one option may seem as good as another, and it's not till the results of the options start rolling in that one may know which way the road will travel. Sometimes, it can be enriching, sometimes it can be frustrating, but the fact is that learning to deal with grey is also a fact of life. It is a determining feature of life as it flows. What remains to be worked for is the ability to handle areas that are short of predictive validity, and yet we need to have the confidence that whatever one does, will have certain predictable fallouts. It is the inability to be predictable of the nature of the fallouts that is the tricky question. It is there when the maturity and ability to grow with life becomes a critical factor. No matter how well one does it, there are huge distances to cover.

Fortunate are the people who believe in reincarnation because it's a continuum, something without a beginning, something without an end — and that itself is the essence of the flow of life. Predictive validity has only one certainty — if anything is certain at all, life goes on, on its own. It needs no crutches, it needs no cheerleaders, it is its own logic.

Professions and Professionals

What this chapter is, also, about

For most people, their professional journey during the initial 10 years will focus on one discipline, or if they are lucky, two disciplines. However, this specialization leaves much to be desired in the formation of a well-rounded individual or professional. Each one of us can learn a lot about people from the bureaucrat, about stress from the doctor, and the list could go on ad infinitum. That we don't work in these disciplines, should not be a reason to not learn from them and improve our skills.

The present day and age is a fascinating one. It is a challenge, and uncomfortably unpredictable. One might add, it gives a feeling of so many things changing at such speed in so many directions. It could well take away from a sense of comfort. In another context, a poet had reflected, "What is this life, so full of care. We have no time to stand and stare?" The reference to change above was only partially captured in these poetic lines.

What is being referred to here is the sheer quantum and unpredictability of change, segment by segment, when put together as a cohesive whole.

It has been recognized even in the slowest of change prone systems — that is the bureaucratic system. The government has now factored in a domain of multi-skilled worker at the lowest level of the echelon. Hence, occupational directions of growth, and the sheer pressure to move from one occupation to another is so immense, that if one didn't do it, one could be left in the wilderness. This happens in every domain, perhaps most dramatically in engineering. Decades ago, the world of telecom was moving from Strowger to ESS-2. These were fundamental changes in telecom technology. ITI, then a premier public sector organization, had 2000 engineers, who were trained in Strowger.

A theoretical solution would have been to replace with new breed ESS-2 expert youngsters, and move on with the system. Palpably, this was a solution which could not be accessed because there was the risk of collateral damage to the human element, and human suffering which no organization could weather. To put it simply, it really needed an organization wide plan to redeploy the skills of the engineers, from one technological assumption to another technological assumption. Ironically, this was termed manpower re-deployment. The truth is, no manpower was being redeployed. Only their skills were to undergo a paradigm shift.

It was as good a case as any of creative rebirth, of technological competency. A matrix had to be created. Each engineer category was placed in a box, and a path was drawn to which box he would be moved to after his re-training/re-learning. It took some months, and it worked. It is one of the most successful stories of so called manpower redeployment at the earliest stages of the game. The redeployment story cannot be the burden of the chapter here. It is the message, and the message is — even within a

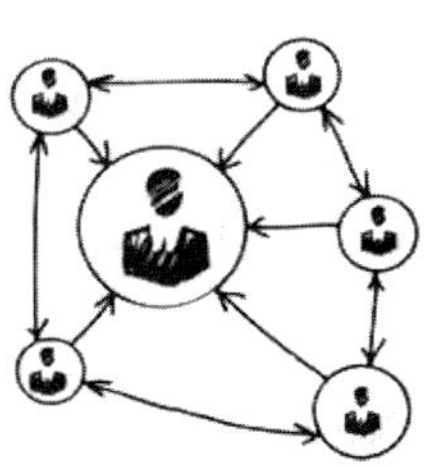

profession, areas have to be shared, and there are fresh areas to venture into.

The story is multiplied many times when it comes to comparison of cross professional characteristics. People usually have a very positive opinion of qualities of their own profession. It's understandable. I recall a director of one of the most successful IITs often punctuating his dialogue when talking to someone, "You know I am an engineer. Ha ha ha! I am very specific. Ha ha ha!" A very self-approving image, and perhaps a valid one for an engineer. Though one must hasten to add, that that's not all that is an engineer. Nor is being specific always a virtue. But there again, that's another story.

In the discursive style in which this chapter has been written, one has to resist the temptations of walking into by-lanes of valid thought. The important thing is to keep the eyes focused clearly on the goals. In this case, what the writing is meant to deal with. This writing is focused on professions and professionals. Put simply, what can one profession learn from another? Take a typical civil servant. In a social conversation, his training as a civil servant would inevitably make him more guarded in offering an opinion. As compared to that, an academic or a journalist will always have an opinion on just about everything, because he makes a living out of commentary. People approach academics for their insights into situations, and listen to their commentary. Similarly, the journalist makes a living not by just peddling the facts, but also, commenting on it. As any sociologist knows, commentary is an art. It requires extensive training, learning, and often a mentor to serve as a sounding board. Making sensible, valid, relevant, pithy comments does not come easy. It's another matter that an increasingly large number of people try their hand at it. Especially, if you are higher at the level of the organization, then one has a tendency to look at one's comments as the utterings of sir oracle.

The professionals who are clearly not on the same page would be engineers, litterateurs, auditors, doctors, seamen, aviators, and the list is as long as the services mankind needs. Thus, it is that the training of an engineer differs from the training of a doctor. That the training differs is not the same thing as saying that there is nothing to learn from each other.

Typically, no doctor is registered as a doctor, or granted a license to practice medicine unless he has completed a given period of internship in a hospital under the necessary supervision of a qualified doctor. Usually, this spreads over a year. The engineer has no such caveat in his career. The moment he finishes his credit requirements, or obtains the percentage required in the final semester; he is considered a qualified engineer. He is even given a provisional degree barring the confirmed of a regular degree. The obtaining of a provisional degree usually does not take even a week. The just born engineer is keen to possess one, and the institution is keen to disperse one. When anxieties meet, a perfect combination emerges, and engineers multiply in numbers without the intervening period that doctors have in their career of internship.

The profession of chartered accountants has a similar caveat. There is a period of articleship before a person is accepted as a practicing chartered accountant. Usually, this is the period of agony, demanding much patience in dealing with many qualities of the seniors, which the apprentice is so, so keen to get off his back. Unfortunately, the situation cannot be helped because statutory provisions make it difficult for it to be handled differently. These are the technicalities. Such extended learning periods with the precursor of different professional backgrounds obviously create typologies of personality. The engineer is more likely than not to see the world, and communicate in a mathematical language of symbols. That's the way he goes.

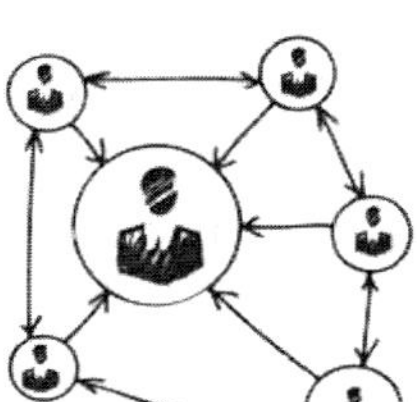

Even emotions, in a lighthearted way, would

be understood much better if put in the framework of circuits and completion of circuits. This is not particularly helpful in dialogue of engineers with other professions. The engineer refers to much of social sciences and humanities as "blah blah blah". The compliments are, of course, generously reciprocated. The net loss is to the user who even in engineering situations has a social context to deal with. So, some of the engineering institutions have tried to compensate for this gap by mounting courses such as human factors in engineering. For this, they have generously granted 3 credits which in some IIT systems would mean roughly around 30 hours of work, and about 120 hours of preparation. If someone believes that 150 hours of learning is enough to get a feel and insight into the world of human social sciences and humanities, one can only evoke god's blessings on his innocence. However, no one seems particularly to mind it. Every inch of resource in engineering institutions is preserved and protected for engineering learning. Even while making some grudging concessions to subjects such as physics, chemistry, mathematics, the approach is not always of generous appreciation of the strengths of those disciplines, but rather a grudging concession to what the discipline has grown to be faced with.

The difference between a scientist and an engineer is not that big, if one takes away from the applied component of an engineering discipline. The area of thermodynamics in electrical engineering is so close to the study of thermodynamics in physics that specialists in this area have sometimes moved from the physics department to the electrical engineering department (the reverse flow is not that common). That is because the social standing of an engineer is higher than the social standing of a scientist. This is because of the employability of an engineer which is higher in public eye to that of a science graduate or post-graduate.

Then, there is a question of self-image. The

engineer is widely recognized to have a very positive self-image. One must hasten to add, so do many other professions. Only in the case of an engineer, a popularly held belief is, "An engineer can do anything". He fancies himself as a planner, a management man, and as an executioner (the pun in the last word is entirely unintended). Hence, engineering institutions, at least the more popular ones, are remarkably closed to the non-engineering domain. If one were to look at an arts or a social sciences institution, one would find that their self-image is also flattering, but is not always deemed productive. Thus, it is that the supreme arbiter of social hierarchy, the Indian mother in law, prefers a son-in-law or daughter-in-law with better earning capacities, where, of course, the engineer ranks higher than the social scientists or humanities specialist.

The story doesn't end there. Professions convert themselves into social hierarchies and professions go through phases. The dream of the Indian mother-in-law in the 60s was an engineer. The dream then accommodated the civil servant through the 70s and the 80s. By the time the 90s came, the corporates were entering the employment domain of the country in a far larger manner than before, and the search began of in-laws working with multinationals, or with successful linkages abroad. It was few people's dream, if any, to get a daughter or son-in-law from a public sector company.

To cut a long story short, professions do have their characteristics, their own ratings, and indeed, their own USPs. In the crucible of social perceptions and norms, it is difficult to go much beyond recording the general lay of the land, but what professions can learn from each other is, and remains, a far more subtle and a basic question. Each profession with its USP which can be a source of inspiration for another profession with a different USP, making it a source of learning.

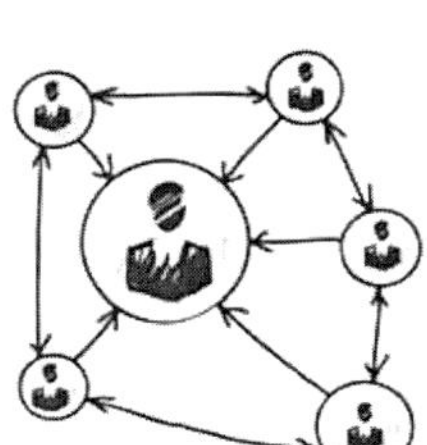

The issue of sustainability requires a humanistic approach. For example, a social science insight to assess where the road is headed, and an engineer's skill to do something about it can make certain things sustainable. It's difficult to conceive of a person who would have all the toolboxes of all these professions rolled into one. However, that is precisely the case for collaborative action and learning from each other, which is a core issue of growth in life.

At the early stage of a learning curriculum, what the educational institutions can do is enable an ability to appreciate others' strength, and a willingness to enrich one's own competencies with those the other profession carries. This is not just a functional requirement, but a much more constructive way of life having in its fold the collective happiness and well-being of all who have to live together as human beings.

There are things beyond professions, say typically a clinical sense. The word comes from the medical sciences. No course in an MBBS curriculum or any other medical degree teaches clinical sense. It is acquired through practice and the ability to understand figures, data, objective reality, and putting it together in a creative interaction to understand, and edit its implications. It's needed in consulting. It may sound strange, but it's also needed in creative writing, which is problem focused. It helps one to treat symptoms and interpret figures in a real world context. There is always so much to learn from another profession because each profession has its USP. Perhaps, the day will come when the chant in the name of interdisciplinary perspective, and multidisciplinary learning would have thrown up some approaches on how one profession can learn from another in a more structured and operational manner.

Collaborations

What this chapter is, also, about

The most challenging problems and exciting domains today are at the intersection of various faculties, and cannot be understood, much less solved, within the boundaries of any single faculty. Therefore, most professionals implicitly understand the importance of collaboration. However, this chapter sheds new light on the importance of collaboration, and its criticality for success.

Some decades ago, when consulting in India was neither fashionable nor remunerative, the understanding of consulting as a profession was limited, and at best, partial. Those were the days when a large number of industry captains were either in Bombay or in Ahmedabad. The leading names were many, and the family of Sarabhai stood tall, not just in Gujarat, but in the vanguard of having enterprises to whom it was expected the future would belong. Sarabhai chemicals were one of the many firms. Ahmedabad Textile Industries Association (ATIRA), now alas almost forgotten, was in the vanguard. People like Prakash Tandon strode in and out of ATIRA shaping what it did, and monitoring what it didn't. A K Rice was to be appointed as a consultant of ATIRA. Promptly, a spate of rumblings were generated. ATIRA was supposed to be too successful an organization to need a consultant. This may not be the best place to go into the merits and demerits of the debate, but broadly, it meant contending with the proposition that appointment of a consultant was recognition of a weakness. Prakash Tandon contested this point of view. The writer of these lines recalls having once read a piece on the subject, where in an interview Prakash Tandon went into the pros and cons of this debate. That was another story.

Years later, in IIT Delhi, in the late 70s, there was a proposal to start a management wing. Sudhir Kakkar was to lead this initiative, and the first external faculty appointed for this program under the leadership of Sudhir Kakkar was the writer of these lines. Soon after joining, the writer expressed a wish to undergo a formal training in creativity and innovation. Promptly, a hornet's nest was stirred. At least one colleague from the industrial engineering department talked to whoever he could speak to ask a very simply question, "What kind of faculty is IIT Delhi appointing if they want to undergo training?" The matter reached the Director. The Director called the coordinator of the management program and the writer and posed this question to them. The writer had a simple point of view, "I was appointed to the institute after due processes of screening, and therefore, it's not for me to say what kind of faculty is being recruited by IIT. However, I reserve the right to ask for training in areas where I think the future of the program may lie, and I may need some inputs. This will have to be the prerogative of anyone. Training inputs are not necessarily a fallout of deficiency." Sudhir Kakkar had an even stronger point of view, and he said, "It's for the institute to make up its mind, and we can't go responding to every single opinion of this order." The subsequent conversation

is unnecessary to produce. The writer went to the training program in question, and that was it.

Be it A K Rice in ATIRA, or the management group in IIT Delhi, the steps, the processes, and the questions have a remarkable similarity. It is perhaps an indicator of the state of art in the domain of management of knowledge. A consultant, as the profession recognizes in many parts of the world, is hired for his specialized domain knowledge, or at times, to save organizational time, or still others, to build upon strengths of exposure to cross-firm operations. Even singly, it's enough to justify the hiring of a consultant, and it nowhere suggests an acknowledgement of a deficiency. The relationship between the two has to be clearly understood to take the narrative forward. Acknowledgement of a deficiency, though by itself not an undesirable thing, is at the best an attempt to bridge an inadequacy.

The reason for hiring a consultant is, however, *suo moto* a constructive effort at collaboration and optimization. In the second case, the reference is to training. Of the many positive reasons for wanting to undergo an orientation or a training is the opportunity it gives for a collaborative thinking in a group mode, while reflecting upon a similar topic of interest to all. Usually, a person with domain specificity leads the discussion, at times, guides it, at times, learns from it, and at times is just a bystander. The learning group or a training group, if you must call it so, acquires its own dynamics. It is not an educational session, say, in the sense that, a first year class in physics, chemistry, or maths maybe.

It is clear that in both the cases, the principle of collaboration

is so rare in the knowledge domain to enable a constructive exchange, that it is still not so recognized universally is an obvious fallout of the narrative above. This is perhaps the strongest roadblock to collaborative activity. A sheer cognitive inability to understand the dynamics of knowledge, and one might add, skill management. To create a true atmosphere of collaboration, one must have the confidence to know what one knows, and the wisdom to recognize what one doesn't. And above all, the ability to source knowledge from where it can be obtained, and have the tools of learning.

These are the foundations of collaboration. The resistance to it comes in many forms. Amongst the more notable ones is a faith in the primacy of one's own discipline. Single disciplinary institutions are particular victims of this. Mercifully, not all in these institutions have a myopic view, but several of them do. Many engineers are convinced of the primacy of engineering. Many auditors don't find any profession as significant as auditing. The environmentalists focus upon environment studies as the end all and be all of existence. The medicine man believes there would be no world without medicine. And of course, the humanities and social scientist position themselves at the fulcrum where purpose and reality meet.

The description can be extended. But in all cases, the core discipline is the loser. It's difficult to think of an engineer managing the engineering profession better than an engineer with a management orientation. The position is simple. The engineer, by himself, is a competent designer of a system. The engineer with a management orientation knows how to put the system to productive use. This is the proposition which has been put forth in at least one of the essays in this book earlier on too. And, the repetition is based on the need of the topic, in this case, collaboration.

Collaboration only strengthens the basic orientation. Collaboration, at a very basic level, enables the person to hear his own echoes, and recognize that disciplinary purity is one thing, and disciplinary wholeness is quite another.

To move the argument further, in an era of emerging disciplines and transforming subject domains of knowledge, experience, and interpretation, there is almost nothing which can happen without constructive collaboration amongst complementary disciplines. In the collaboration between engineering and social sciences, environment maybe one aspect of the discussion. Quite another is the need to realize that most disciplines in their own right have become interdisciplinary in their essential nature, thereby making collaboration a core principle. Take civil engineering for example. A course on public hygiene and deep sea mining may have little in common, but they are brought together under the rubric of civil engineering. It is the collaborative principle which holds it together. If there is a commonality of underlying principles and assumptions, quite apparently disparate branches can emerge with a regular identity of their own, yet requiring collaboration to be operationally successful.

The foundations of the response to this need have to be laid early in life by helping the learner to see the essential unity of knowledge and the collaborative character of human existence. To move the understanding of the subject matter forward, one needs to reflect on the nature of the family, the nature of institutional growth, the character of dyadic relationships, and interpersonal dynamics. In each case, collaboration is the basic underlying principle. It's all very well to have unisex parlours and unisex dress habits, and to do away with gender prejudices. But the bottom line is that any two individuals have to collaborate, if they have to deal with each other. Sometimes, putting an argument at its simplest level helps, and collaboration is needed even in communication. If two people talk together, neither can hear what the other person is saying. And if the other person cannot be heard, why should something be said?

Collaboration is as basic as that, but for this, seeds of understanding of one's own strengths and knowing one's own needs have to be sown early. Collaboration is not only essential to life, but is at the core of existence itself.

It doesn't take too much of knowledge or wisdom to realize that there is cosmic collaboration and universal collaboration in the laws of nature to let the universe move forward without accident of planets hitting each other, or generating a turmoil through chaotic, unbridled movements. Collaboration needs discipline. Collaboration needs insights. Collaborations need foresight.

Collaboration between the living and the non-living, collaboration amongst the species, and indeed collaboration amongst the contending aspirations within oneself is the roadmap of existence and universe, especially amongst human beings. The truth is simple: whether we like it or not, we need each other.

Tripwires

What this chapter is, also, about

In any career, the temptation to obtain outsized returns for minimal effort are many. Which of these is a tripwire, and which is not, is a matter of judgement and context. However, this chapter lays out a strong case of how to contextualize decisions, and have an internal compass while navigating such decisions.

Life is full of two kinds of situations. The first one is the last gamble which one decided to take, and was stumped. It is also full of stories of how one believes because to believe is a fundamental need. That belief in that one person who decided to change and exchange the relationship for a seeming comfort ruined the relationship while destroying faith.

The fascinating fallout of these two observations is the belief that it won't happen to me. Studies on HIV or for that matter, any other disaster, is quite often rooted in the belief that disaster happens to others, not to oneself. Of the many human capacities, the most enigmatic one is the capacity for self-deception. Yet, the printed word, and the visual depictions of success on the screen hold out almost universally the principle, or need for which Robespierre proclaimed during the French revolution, "Audacity, Audacity, still more audacity," to achieve one's goals.

The charmed narratives don't end there. Read any set of biographies. Half of them are descriptions of people who dropped out of school, who failed to make the grade, who made abominable errors, and yet did that one thing right which brought them fame, or had them hit the jackpot. The upshot of all this is really quite confusing at an impressionable age, and a tender mind.

Part of growing up is about looking for replicable examples and experiences. If Rabindranath Tagore could be a celebrity poet despite never going to a school, or if Bill Gates could setup the world's largest IT empire after being a college dropout; then surely there is little merit in completing school or college. A palpably false proposition because life by imitation is life full of inundation. If Rabindranath Tagore was a model of what happens to those not enrolling in schools , then that would be an even bigger model. And if Bill Gates' rise to success is the roadmap of achievement, then all colleges should be closed down. Clearly a proposition which will have very few takers.

So, one ends up with the inevitable query, where lies the truth?

It is important to realize that not everyone can be Bill Gates or Rabindranath Tagore. There is just far too much talk of dramatic success, or far too much deference to dramatic failure. For a vast majority of the species of homo-sapiens, life is essentially a simple proposition of meeting the essential needs of human existence, having four square meals a day, a roof over one's head, and relatively healthy life to get through the living years without tripping up.

The tripwires are many. They come in the form of: "I can be great too, and for that, I have to break the rules just once". Obviously, one can think of someone in one's own domain of experience who got away with it. What one forgets is that for every one that got away with it; there are literally hundreds upon thousands of people who didn't. The social reprisal of them is unforgiving. Witness the avalanche of criminal cases in court, and the teeming numbers behind bars. Life is about recognizing that everyone is not born to be a genius, and indeed, there is no need to be one.

A reasonably trouble free life on the front of health, career, conjugal, and family harmony with sometime to enjoy the bounties of nature, and the blessings of God, and coasting without too much fretting to a normal healthy end is perhaps a boon not to be easily sneered at.

There is no justification for every single human being on this planet wanting to be a celebrity of one variety or another. This is where the Indian philosophy steals a march over everything else. It places internal peace beyond all achievements. Indian folklore, history, legends, and narratives are full of characters, men and women, who knew how to give rather than hanker after having more. India is perhaps the only culture, where abandonment of material pursuits for great achievement of physical and emotional peace has been chronicled in every era with such detail, if nowhere else, in oral history.

It is another matter that historians, as a profession, haven't woken up to this reality of Indian evolution, and the history books are full of narratives of kings, and one almost said, cabbages. It is the subtle glorification, and the not so subtle display of wealth as

an objective that has led to the kind of seething bedlam in the streets, in the offices, in schools, and in colleges, not to forget homes, and transport vehicles. It seems somewhat odd, that notwithstanding the universal adulation of Vivekanand or Mohandas Karamchand Gandhi, not one Indian mother holds the ideal of making her child yet another Vivekananda or Mohandas Karamchand Gandhi.

The dream of an Indian mother is a multi-degree holder child , successful in a profession, which accesses wealth, influence, and which shortcuts the harassment of queues, columns, and multiple responses for fulfilment of requests, which in many places outside India, is a routine matter. Interestingly, no political party, even remotely talks of this. In fact, the recent elections had the not so rare sight of two major political parties of this country offering largesse to farming communities to the tune of 72000 rupees, or 6000 rupees. The variations of the amount doesn't really matter, because in the equation, there was also a variation of the number of recipients, the total coming to broadly the same. Clearly politics has its own ways. That is another story.

Sticking to the issue of tripwires, and reflecting upon what constitutes success, and what are role models; it is difficult to overlook the fact that most success stories of many brilliant narratives have at the heart of it some violation of some ethical principle, which many talk about, but everyone claims that it was never proven. Yet, success builds its own narratives, and its own contributions. This is totally understandable.

The strange thing about success is its inconsistency. Many people who are successful in one decade become controversial in another. There is no industrial empire which has lasted even 200 years. The oldest organization on this planet is perhaps the Church of Rome, or other older ones being the *vihars* which the Buddhists established. But no political empire survived. It's very difficult to find a biography of a successful man with no controversy.

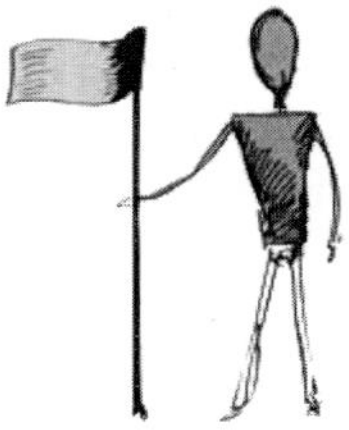

Be that as it may, the fact remains of an enigma which accompanies the search for a roadmap of success. The governmental sector is often seen as wayward by many, though the governmental sector has more watchdogs and regulatory agencies than any other sector. How do these contradictions co-exist? If there any research has been done on this, the results are still to be known. It has been mentioned in the preceding lines that the basic search is for the narrative and the roadmap for success for an individual who is unlikely to be the CEO of a mega-industrial empire, or a political leader commanding great respect, and having many followers, or indeed a scholar, who will make such contributions as to remembered the way Meghnad Saha or Einstein are. The tripwires which come along one's way are in the form of small temptations, and hope for large profits at the end of it; built on a sub-structure of a belief that if so many have got away with it, so can I.

There is no coherent response to this kind of analytical approach. Yet, like many analytical approaches, it has its own contradictions. The contradiction is wanting success and praying for it on standards which others achieved without developing one's own insights, or one's own ability to redeem and fulfill. It also has other huge gaps. A singular lack of belief in a very simple fact which has proven itself in multiple ways, multiple times, namely there is a moral law in the world. Pages of history, of conquests, and biographies of successful people are replete with indications which show that there is a force beyond calculations, and a might beyond power and authority.

Why did Hannibal stand at the gates of ancient Rome at the head of the mighty army of Carthage when Rome was full of old men, women, and children, the younger ones either out in the field or killed, and do nothing? Hannibal could have entered the city, pillaged, and ravaged it; but decided to turn back. Who and what explains this? There are many such stories, even political history, an arbiter of conflict seem to be decided by what they call the hinge factor. Indeed, if the

hinge factor is all that important, what is the place of successful calibrated and pliant pursuit of material goals?

These are questions which are raised in some history classes, but the scientific method, creating a value of its own doesn't want to touch it with a barge pole. It maybe all to the good; but it demonstrates what the scientific method cannot explain. If the scientific method cannot explain, does it become untrue? Similarly, to stray from the straight path is as difficult as the realization of the limits of one's own faculties, capacities, and potential for growth. Above all, any existence bound by time began at a point of time, and shall end at the end of his time. Time does not pass, it is the person which passes. Hence, it's difficult to justify a quest for achieving more than the simple straightforward route.

The trip-up factors of personal deceit, of that one attempt to do what you know should not ever have been attempted, and that one betrayal releases a cosmic energy which cannot either be measured or tracked. Sometimes it comes back, sometimes it doesn't. Because it doesn't come back even once, it cannot become a message to others of replicable behavior. It does come back sometimes ‾ when it does come back, it does so with a vengeance. The hopeful deviant then seeks solace in the philosophy that it cannot happen to me. The hinge factor itself has no logic, other than saying it is a logic which has not yet been grasped by human intelligence.

The tripwires come in many forms. The easiest is financial impropriety, and of the course, the most common one is gender liaison. The grief that either has caused still awaits a scientific documentation and understanding of causative factors. People learn of such cases, and smile with smugness of the testimony to their own intelligence, and how they will never be the victims of stumbling over such tripwires. This is rooted in a very common belief, which perhaps most human beings have

– a total faith and ultimate conviction of their being smart at a level and scale which people have not even begun to understand.

Why else would one lie? Everyone lies. And everyone who lies, lies in the belief that he will get away with it because he is smarter than the person listening. That is the most universal tripwire. Yes, they exist. Looking for them with a torch may not help. But the light of wisdom might just work. There is no wisdom in tackling the tripwire, but there is great peace in not having anything to do with it.

Mentorship

What this chapter is, also, about

Mentorship is a layered process, and a journey of discovery. This chapter hints, but does not reveal all that is needed. This pointer is critical for someone to understand mentorship beyond the usual application of the word. It reads as if there is more to come, and encourages the reader to go on a journey of self-discovery. Like any other good text, it alludes to the possible, but does not dictate all that there is. It indicates, rather than mandates. And equally importantly, it enables the reader to differentiate between the myth and the reality of finding a mentor.

The word school has different meanings in different contexts. One obvious meaning of a school is where children go to study. Another usage of a school which is popular, but perhaps less common, is an approach to a thought or a problem, so is referred to as a school of thought. This is common in philosophy, political theory, economics, and almost any branch of learning. The word school is used for a group of fishes who swim together, presumably because of certain affinity. School as a word has overtones of learning, thinking, pursuit of knowledge, and anything to do which has overtones of knowledge management. In each case, there is a person who knows better, and a person who seeks to learn. Different culture idioms have different concepts of learning, assumptions of learning, and indeed processes of learning.

In the Indian school of thought, the status of a guru, freely translated as master, is beyond question. It is very different from the Newtonian school of learning, where inquiry is the driving urge. One is supposed to question, again question, and question still further, almost till the point where there are more questions than possible answers. Then, the learner feels triumphant. The purpose of this narrative is not to comment on this approach, and still less to resolve it. There is a virtue in being descriptive, and leaving it to the judgement of the receiver to resolve the issue to his satisfaction. The vantage point of understanding lies in the fact that very often the cognitive limits of the person making the inquiry is as much a determinant of the solution, as the cognitive levels of the person responding to the inquiry. One accepts a solution which fits into the framework of understanding of the person with the query.

The above narrative may not solve all the possible crests and troughs of the learning process, but it highlights a simple truth. The truth is learning is a complicated process in which there are at least three players ‾ the learner, the context, and the process of learning. The teacher, the facilitator in the modern idiom is often considered an optional extra. The focus of the parade is on the first person singular pronoun ‾ I, me, my, and the list can go on. The statements can be: "I don't agree"; "I don't see the point";

"In my point of view"; "In my experience"; "My way of looking at things". This ad nauseum drumming up of the self is perhaps the biggest impediment of learning, because if one is so wise, then one should know it all. Unfortunately, modern emphasis on technology, to put it mildly, has done very little to mitigate this aberration.

It is a bewildering experience to see a whole school of thought emerging which believes in letting the learner search his knowledge even if he is a 10 year old child. The celebration of the redundancy of a teacher has created a whole school of thought of child's education, which understandably encourages him to explore, but does not want to give the benefit of any experience. Imagine, the theory of self-explanation being used as an alibi to re-discover the laws of physics from heat to light. We would have groups of 7-10 years old, running around the ground, striking stone against each other to find out if it generated any heat or produced any light. Nothing wrong with that, but it would hardly fit in with different levels of knowledge, which humans need as they grow from childhood to teenage, and adulthood, middle age, senior level of age, and further periodization of human life can add to more stages of learning requirements.

Given the limitations of this text, and the time that would be spent in reading it, it would be simpler to say that like in everything else, the middle path is the best way of learning processes. Of course, exploration and experimentation should be encouraged. But by the same token, imbibing the wisdom of preceding sentinels of learning, and using that as a benchmark of going forward cannot be trivialized.

Mentorship is that magical process which bridges these seemingly mutually exclusive approaches together. Mentorship is about learning, about trusting another person's experience, knowledge, insight, affection, and responsibility to trust his words, and to find out where to search. If all learning were to be about de novo experiences and discovery of everything on its own, then human life would be too short a span of any learning or discovery beyond what was already not known or accepted before.

In Indian ethos, all learning is supposed to begin with that word, *"Aapt vachan..."* A free translation of the word *aapt* is faith. A free translation of *"Aapt vachan"* would be the word of faith. One trusts someone for no better reason that this someone is one who can be trusted, and is known to be knowledgeable.

How does one know somebody is knowledgeable? It is like love. No matter how literate and profound advertising literature may appear, there are no real indicators of love. Somebody can love by yelling out of concern. Another person can be totally silent in love, because of a feeling of hurt. A third can love by pouring oneself out to the point where the recipient begins to feel throttled. Standardization of manifestations of love are so many that it would be almost impossible to catalog them, and yet one knows when one is in love, or when somebody loves them.

The role of feeling, experience, and understanding has been so underplayed in the learning processes that it has been almost eliminated in the structured training of a learner. No B.Ed. course, no training of trainers program, no conclave of educationists seems to dwell upon this. There is so much emphasis on use of electronic methods of exchange of information, satellite networks, or internet of things that one almost begins to believe that this is the sole universe. One must hasten to add that *suo motu* learning enabled by technology is nothing wrong. But to attribute to it virtues of universal completeness, so as to leave no space of any alternate method of learning, can be as suicidal as ignoring technologically enabled learning.

The mentor through his experience, insight, learning, and foresight is able to almost instinctively feel his way through this seductive jungle of competing enticements. That's where a mentor becomes indispensable to the narrative. A mentor is not needed only in that act and scene; he is needed elsewhere. A mentor is needed when the mind is covered with fog. A mentor is needed when the heart loses its compass. A mentor is needed in transitioning from one reality to another. A mentor is needed in the discovery of one's own self. A mentor is needed where in every other place, there are limits imposed by resources of learning.

There is a welcome move in certain segments of corporate quarters to institutionalize mentoring. This happens every so often in induction processes, in rough patches of interpersonal relations, and walking through the difficult terrain of restated strategic perspectives.

But above all, being a mentor or looking for a mentor is like being in love, or looking for that existential experience which is beyond the arithmetic or algebraic equations. Almost at the risk of sounding unscientific, and at times one has to be unscientific, to one struggling through life, finding a mentor can be a matter of chance, or simply a matter of being open to another person's experiences and wisdom.

It is an alchemy, which so far, has not been put in an algorithm, or in an equation of navigation. It is the essence of the experience of life, and having faith in the laws of nature, if that be the phrase with highest acceptability of the largest number that each one has a path of happiness and fulfilment waiting for him. The mentor is the guide who will emerge, at a time and place of his own choosing, at times without he himself knowing that he is going to become a mentor to someone. It is these little so called accidents of life which impart to life a mystery. A mystery being a word used to label a process or a situation which the limits of human cognition is not fully able to grasp.

Mentorship can be spiritual, can be emotional, can be scientific, can be everywhere where the search for the next level of growth is seen as the very purpose of life. Accordingly, mentorship is a point of evolution in relationships, where care is the foundation. One of the most charming aspects of mentorship emerges not only when a senior mentors a junior, or a precocious junior mentors a senior (recall the wisdom of a 4 or 5 year old which bewilders the grown-ups). Mentorship is also between equals. Mentorships takes turns. Mentorship is a question of providing the light when the other person needs it, and a helping hand when the other person feels weak, or even holding his fingers to lead the other person gently forward, when he feels the encircling doom, and almost wants to give up because life does not seem to respond the way one would want it to.

Mentorship is about hope. It is a craft, it is a gift of nature, of caring people being with each other, because together each one becomes better than being singly tormented by the surprises which life so profusely springs at unexpected times, at unexpected corners.

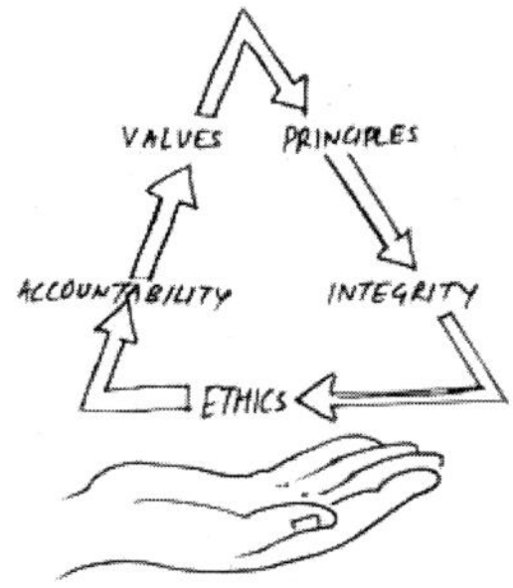

Corporate Ethics

Why one should read this chapter?

It is the rare person who has not violated some norm of ethics, written or unwritten, knowingly or unknowingly at some point of time. Most justify it to themselves with the adage, "the circumstances demanded it". Yet, many also know this is a slippery slope. For the circumstances will demand it again, and again. Anyone who did not do the right thing once, will be doubly tempted to test his/her luck the second time. That's when the law of averages starts catching up. At some point or the other, either the person's greed or luck runs out. Unfortunately, the latter is more prevalent than the former.

This chapter helps a person understand what constitutes corporate ethics, and why they are important. It also highlights the relationship between ethics, and one of the most important aspects of professional life ‑ personal branding. Those in professional services (doctors, lawyers, accountants, architects etc.) would already be familiar with this. But for the others, it would suffice to say that personal branding is what helps differentiate the great from the merely good, and is a critical aspect in one's ascent to the top. And ethics is the secret sauce that differentiates legendary brands from the transient ones.

P.S. If one was to memorize a single line from this chapter, this would be it: "Essential to functioning, necessary to live up to, tempting to violate, and yet capable of deadly tripping when one least expects it."

There is the story of this person who was working in a government institution of training, and was the beneficiary of an exchange program of six months with MIT. Since that person could speak fluent English, and had the power of expression, the selectors decided to let that person enjoy the benefit of the opportunity. To get to the essence of the matter, that person was allowed to go abroad with the clear understanding that he was to serve for three years upon return from training there. On return, the brand of MIT made that person what all persons with foreign training have experienced, a visible entity in peer groups. The opportunity was used to send applications all around, quietly do the interviews, don a fake smile, and get into an institute of national importance. Predictably, the chicken came home to roost. The prime mover of the recruitment, who till that moment was oblivious of the obligation this person had jumped, decided to give the benefit of the doubt, and bailed the person out of a possible loss of job, if not a career setback.

The person repaid the compliment with a vengeance in subsequent years, and became an expert in ethics. This is a story from personal experience. For obvious reasons the identity is not being discussed. It doesn't make a difference to the narrative. This type is fairly common, and people are known to get away with such slipshod behavior. Ethics has become like modesty, but then it's also abused like modesty. Modesty is an essential ingredient of human experience, but it's also a way, which helps one to be a better self. Displayed and flaunted, it becomes counterproductive, and becomes a tool of attempted social recognition.

Ethics is something similar. It helps one to stay straight, walk straight, and keep the system lubricated with the essentials of faith, decency, and correctness. One must recognize that rules, regulations, and norms which create a benchmark of what is a cognizable offence and unacceptable. However, it only goes so far. Beyond it is a whole universe of basic human decency, correctness, and integrity, which governs everything written, and often what is unwritten.

Consider the ability of the roof to stay put ¯ the ceiling under which the reader is seated while reading these pages. Usually, the last thought in the mind of the reader would have been to ask oneself, the probability of the roof holding while that person sat in the room. The unstated assumption is the completion certificate of that room must have been given after due processes, and that it must have been obtained. It occurs to no one that colonies are known to have several unauthorized constructions, but not too many people bother about. So, the question of completion certificate of that unauthorized room would not arise. Even if it was authorized, and there was a completion certificate required, no one would seriously doubt the authenticity or the correctness of the construction of the room. The completion certificate must have been given correctly. There rests the matter. It is assumed that the professional ethics were followed.

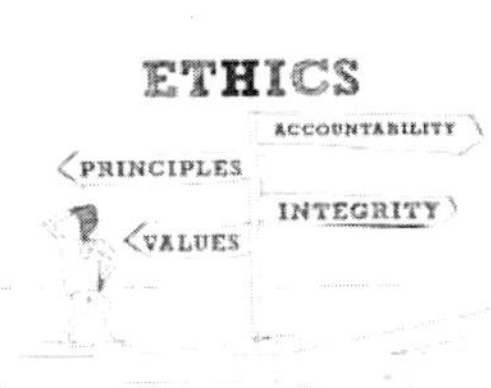

Truly speaking, there isn't much of a choice either. How many completion certificates can one ask for? Extending the analogy further, the story gets even more interesting. How does one know that the pilot of the aircraft which one is boarding is not inebriated? Or that the breath test of the pilot was duly and correctly administered? How does one know whether the water one has ordered in an eatery is hygienically sound? How does one know what one has bought has labels which are not recycled?

Even if one had the tools of cross-checking, the number of cross-checking and the frivolity of it would be so great that life would become fairly impossible. Hence, the obvious conclusion, faith is fundamental to life. This is true in matters big and small. Not many children have an opportunity to have their father undergo a paternity test. The word of their mother on fatherhood is considered sacrosanct, final, and beyond doubt. It lets the society work in peace, and the cornerstone again is faith. Whether it is integrity, risk, or belief, the roots are in ethics. Hence, ethics is to life what oxygen is to keeping a person alive. Philosophizing over ethics is akin to a meandering dream which would have no beginning and no end.

However, the time to say amen has not yet arrived. Everywhere, just as ethics is endemic, pushing of boundaries of ethics is also endemic. The conman survives on it. It's the rare person who has not overpaid, or has not been shortchanged. It means the same thing, but the processes are different. Hence, all professions talk of ethics. Some of them even have an oath attached at the end of the training, education, at the time of getting of the degree which makes one solemnly swear by ethical conduct, then and forever. Rarely does one get caught because the circumstances are ambiguous, and identifiable evidence is difficult to come by. Riding on the benefit of doubt, many get home unscathed.

Herein lies the catch. The more one succeeds in getting away with it, the more the appetite is whetted. And criminal records have any number of cases where that last one chance was the booby trap which became the final chance. Putting it in simple language, it is the frailty of human nature which prevents one from drawing the line one step short of the precipice, or pushing one's luck too far. This requires judgement and restraint. Indeed, if one has judgement and restraint, one would not walk this path anyhow. Ethics in its corporate incarnation is a different matter altogether.

There are people who believe that one cannot get rich in a visibly displayable manner which arouses the envy of others from saving and making money just through honest means. It is when one succeeds fully, and is visible enough with unearned riches that one becomes celebrated, and the sins are forgiven.

This is a hypothesis difficult to test, but is widely believed. There are people who hold the opposite view with equal aplomb. They believe that no matter how smart one is, unearned income always has a bitter parting, and people simply don't see the correlation. The belief is if you have unearned income, or ethics, then you lose something on the rebound what you have gained on the swing. Typically, there will be sudden illness or sudden departure of a dear one which you would have never wanted to lose to begin with.

These are beliefs which have never been tested in laboratory conditions. People hold them all the same. These are the many manifestations and dimensions of ethics, which touch each and every one of us. Swearing is a typical manifestation of the essential ethics of relationships. If somebody swears by touching the head of somebody near and dear, the chances of his speaking the truth are not 100%, but the percentage of truth there in terms of statements does certainly improve.

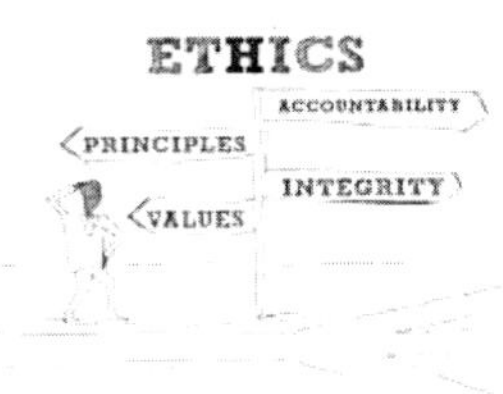

Therefore, belief is the core of ethics. There is in each one of us, a sense of right and wrong, which is ingrained almost automatically, and is not just acquired through socialization. Linking it with the society along some of the foregoing lines, an attempt has been made to indicate how it is the bedrock of all relationships.

In a formal, corporate environment, ethics acquires a unique shape. It begins at the time of signing of a contract, to which punitive clauses, and courts of adjudication are added. There are people who believe that they will sign anything which is put up for their signature in such a mode, because they know that it can't be implemented anyhow. Mercifully, such people are not too many, but it's important to realize that they do exist. The number of times a contract is upheld in an organization is often less than the number of times they are violated. Many people believe in the saintly attributes of forgiveness, giving a second chance, letting people learn are used *ad nauseum* to overlook violations. The purpose of these lines cannot be to sit on judgement over such an approach. But then it becomes a big stick when one wants to use it.

There are other dimensions of corporate ethics, especially when it comes to medicine, auditing, marking of answer scripts, and the list can be added to. In each case, so much depends on the ethics of the practitioner. When the abdomen is open, and a surgery of the intestine is being attempted, what means can be there to check whether the knife that is being used is totally disinfected or not? It is not as if the case of infection through infected knives have not been recorded. And yet one learns to trust because one believes in the doctors adhering to the Hippocratic oath.

Teachers don't have this oath, but they still mark answer scripts. What they mark can make or unmake careers. Whereas there are the usual percentage of aberrations, most of them perform a decent job of the prerogative. So far as this dimension of ethics is concerned, God is in his heaven

and peace is on earth. However, trouble begins when corporate ethics becomes the tool of business enhancement. The client and the consultant can develop a cozy relationship, which together can be used to beat the law. The client can get away with it, and the consultant rakes in the money.

The bad news is such luck runs out sooner or later. If it didn't, there would have been total chaos in the world. It is not as if the culprit has never got away. But then, by and large, the rotation of the earth on its axis, in a manner of speaking, has not yet been disturbed. The dangerous part comes in when corporate ethics becomes a tool of competitiveness, and there are dicey areas where personal ethics and collective ethics intersect. Consider an attractive male, an attractive female coming together in unison, deciding to have happy times together, and one coming from the client group and the other from the consultant group, bonding in a way in which the dominant of the two personalities starts tilting the balance. The agreeability in tilting the balance is seen as a testimony to one's honesty of emotions. It can be called an imperfect potpourri. The casualty is always the corporate well-being of one or the other group.

These incidents are not that rare, and corporate history is dotted with graveyards of enterprises which got away/ nearly did/ nearly did not and totally sank. Consider the case of Enron, consider the case of Rajat Gupta. The stories are far too well known to need a recount. But people who have read Rajat Gupta's writings after his release from jail are often left wondering whose fault it was, and what purpose did the law serve? Yes, it served as a deterrent for the faint hearted for whom going to jail is a nightmare. There are also the species who believe that going to jail for a while is worth it, because when the jail sentence finishes, what is available for spending can be so much larger

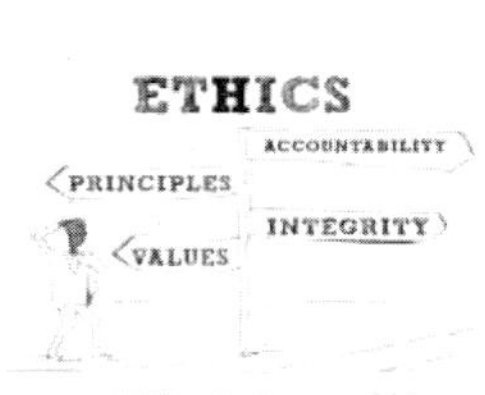

than what one would have got by saving. The purpose of this narrative cannot be to explain away a course of action which is *apriori* unacceptable, and therefore, wrong.

The purpose is to illustrate how alternative mindsets propel unethical behavior. Ethics is always founded on the principle of what you do in the dark, when you know that you cannot get caught, and yet your own sense of correctness is the impediment to pushing the boundary and attempting to alter the logic. Life is full of challenges in the area of corporate ethics, when it comes to promotion, of careers, while negotiating contracts, fulfilling the quality dimension of the contracts, and indeed what one believes is the cornerstone of one's own brand. At the end of the day, the beauty of experience in life is of little episodes with or without evidence in the psyche of the belief of the people which creates a brand. One writes one's own brand, and brand is more often than not true. Like always there is a fly in the ointment. There are people who deliberately create a brand, and indeed live it in many small and larger issues. Then carry out one big violation which nobody would believe they were capable of. This could be truly called reverse branding in action.

No matter how one plays it, there is no perfect system, and corporate ethics is like ethics anywhere. Essential to function, necessary to live up to, tempting to violate; yet, capable of deadly tripping when one least expects it. It is not for gamblers, that is a different profession. Corporate ethics keeps the profession going, and it enables one to have that intangible feeling of satisfaction, peace of mind, and ultimately, peace within oneself, as one moves from one unknown to another unknown. In a strange way, personal ethics is the bedrock of corporate ethics.

Hence, it all goes back essentially to the way people are recruited, trained, and oriented to manage their aspirations. It is as much a matter of belief, as the possibility of getting away with that lucky dip. It's easy to be a doubting Thomas when it comes to corporate ethics, but impossible to survive without it. And that is the power of truth. Even lies have to parade as truths to gain acceptability.

Personal ethics, collective ethics, corporate ethics is what makes it possible for civilization to function and survive. Wisdom of people who believe it is an optional extra has been known to be disastrous in many ways which can be explained, and some which cannot be explained. If by and large, fatherhood is a matter of belief, necessity of corporate ethics is much more so. Yes, sometimes a payment slip accompanies it. But then it is a question of which tab one is willing to pick up.

Personal choices, corporate ethics, and the axis of the world going around on an even keel are all self-given truths. To debate it, and to doubt it would leave an endless vacuum to stare at that has no logic, let alone a future to feed itself.

Go Big, Or Go Home

What this chapter is, also, about

The desire to make a big impact in life may vary from person to person. However, for those who do want to make it big, they would be well-advised to remember that it is their mindset that propels growth, and not any other factor (including skillset). This chapter emphasizes that it is not just good, but even desirable to set our own limits, big or small, and consequently, accept the good and the bad arising out of those limits. For many who are running in a corporate rat race, or chasing the next big dream, this should be a sobering thought, and one which causes them to pause and reflect before moving ahead.

There is an *Upanishad* dictum, "*Bhuma vaisukham, alpe sukham nasti*". In a free translation, it means comfort and happiness is by having things in an expansive mode. Little things don't give happiness. A statement like this is calibrated to generate a debate, and the intellectuals, the pseudo-intellectuals, and the unintellectuals all have an opinion on something such as this. In any case, in the Indian subcontinent, almost everyone has an opinion on almost everything. So be it. It's an articulate community, and the basic mindset cannot be grudged. Getting back to the idea of largeness, its concept in a physical sense may be easier to communicate than in a deep philosophical sense.

Gender attraction is as old as human civilization, and there is no record of one gender wooing another with statements such as, "I love you just a little bit", or, "I want a bit of your love", or, "you are clearly far from being the best. But it will do." Examples can be multiplied. The direction it would take is predictable. The common thing is to promise eternity, to promise fullness. To woo by comparisons with the best, the biggest, and the greatest. Moon is a very common metaphor used in everyday parlance. Honey follows closely. Tarts are a common usage. If there is a reference to somebody one likes, it has to be a sweetheart. There certainly isn't any such thing as "Listen my half sweetheart." The intellectualization apart, nobody would want to hear it. Hence, the algorithm is set, and is clear. The fascinating thing is that it is repeated over and over again, and one almost waits for the time to pass through that phase. There is nothing novel in saying, "I love you", but all say it, and all say it more than once in a lifetime.

The message is simple. Joy, fullness, appreciation is in immensity, even at the risk of coining a new word.

Emotions are the first area explored in the domain of "Going big". But it's not confined to emotions. Many would have heard various views on power. Power, like love, cannot be shared. It is shared only to negotiate a larger slice for oneself in face of adversity. Power is often considered a double-edged sword and doesn't, like any other emotion, always have a constructive overtone. The statement, 'Power corrupts, and absolute corrupts absolutely' is a truism. The most powerful people in the

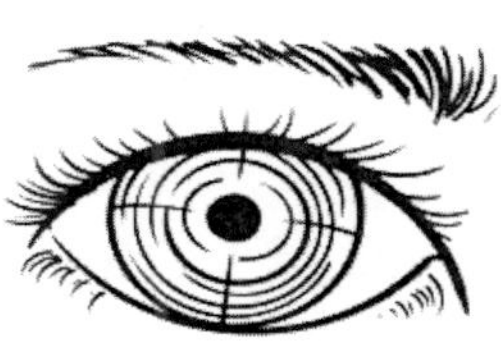

political history of different parts of this planet are the ones which have met strange fates. Talking of Hitler is passé. And Churchill, after having victoriously led the British, could not win a seat in the Parliament at the end of the Second World War. Obviously, something did not gel somewhere.

Be it love, be it power, be it fame, or anything else; the list can be extended *ad nauseum*. One wants more and more and more till it feeds upon itself and reaches the point of being counterproductive. The story of going big, however, is not just that. Bigness, of course, means entirety of the possibility. It means pushing of the potential, and discovering of the latent talents in the individual and in the group. But going big has the strict requirement of high visualization, and going beyond the limits as it were. No one could be thinking big by first reading the rules and regulations. The rules and regulations always follow the dictum of what succeeded, and the lowest common multiple of willingness to accept. A good case in sight whose interpretation is almost exclusively determined by the context is the killing of a human being. In one theatre of action, killing a human being would lead to an investigation, framing of charges, and punishment. The same act of killing an individual in another theatre of action would mean applaud, recognition, and even bestowal of honor. The context defines the regulation. Logic always follows.

If one were to bring a spiritual dimension to bigness, it is easy to correlate it to *vedantic* thought when one believes that each human being has an element of the divine. They are parts of the infinite Creator. Then it follows that Nirvana, or getting out of the cycles of birth and rebirth will only happen when that element of infinity that is found in each living being goes back to merge into the cosmic energy. However, that maybe named.

The purpose of this write up is not to create a parallel living tree with a discourse on spirituality. However, to deny spirituality as an element, and a driver in all and everything which one does is also to deny the pulsation of life. The tendency to deny what one cannot understand comes easy to so called intellectuals. Hence, one rarely sees a serious discussion on the spiritual element in a business decision. In a manner of speaking, business modelling is often attempted in total denial of any spiritual element. Yet, to borrow yet another word from the Sanskrit idiom, any businessman knows that after all the modelling has been done, the SWOT analysis carried out, socio-economic analysis put in place, funds raised, and investments and expenditure forecast, there is always that dimension of *Prarabdha*.

Prarabdha is a difficult word to translate. It has a strong cultural idiom. It is as difficult to explain to a semi-developed mind as it is to explain the poem *Daffodil* to a person who has never seen the daffodil bloom, or even more specifically, the Lake Districts of England. The fond emotion that words translate emotions is best answered by a simple experience which most human beings have of the beloved pleading with the lover while in his arms and a close embrace to let her go and let it be, which only leads to the lover holding her closer in a firmer grasp, and she becomes quite willing to be a party to it. How does one translate this into words? Stylization? Reluctance? Playing difficult? Playing games? A metaphor which means one thing, and says the opposite? Or simply, it doesn't need to be explained because everyone understands?

To the Newtonian inquiring mind, a simple question can be raised, where was all this taught? In the classroom? In early childhood? In group ethics? And if this has to be learnt, who taught whom? In any part of the world at different stages of exploration of a physical relationship, why does femininity always have such similar responses as the male in any part of the world enjoys the game of pursuit?

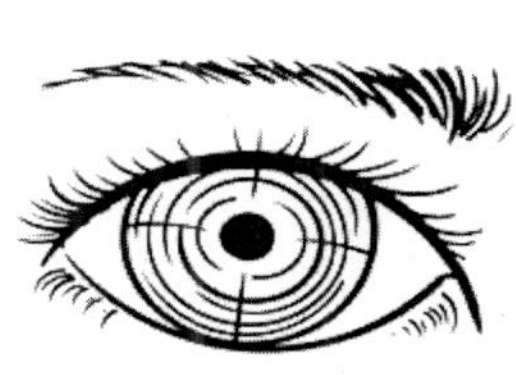

Some do it with poetic flair, others artistically, still others in a stylized manner. Of course, there are any number of people who do it in a vulgar, uncouth, almost a savage manner. But the basic driving instinct of pursuit is always there. All this is never taught. So begins the basic explanation of how much of learning is instinctive, and how much of it is transferrable?

These are big questions. Such big questions that one never gets beyond small answers. Hence, it is that everyone understands what's gong big. However, people will be taught moderation, for which they will be extolled. They will be taught to be happy with what they have. And like in many shades of human experience, there is nothing wrong with that approach any more than there is with any other approach. Yet, going back to the simple principles of creativity and innovation, there is no substitute for thinking big.

It is reported that the first inspiration to fly came to man's mind after watching birds fly. There are records of people who put wings on their hands, jumped out of higher stories, trying to flap their hands, to move the wings they had put on both the hands ¯ faster and quicker ¯ obviously trying to imitate birds, but crashed to the ground. Decades and more of such experimentation led to a very simple solution. When you can't confront the problem, circumvent it. When you can't walk with strength through the enemy, go around it. The infantry strategist will talk of this as a very common approach in troops deployment. But this is not confined to the troops alone. It is applied almost everywhere. When humans learnt that they could neither acquire wings, nor slide their hands or feet into them; they decided to experiment and create a machine which would propel and carry him. Hence was born the aeroplane.

Refining it became necessary because propulsion by propeller went only so far. The jet engine then emerged, and the thinking grew bigger. Man wanted to go beyond the stratosphere and go to another planet. Constant questioning, querying, thinking big, created new territories and new frontiers. So, the rocket was born. One stage rocket, two stage rocket, three stage rocket, and then to keep the load under control, the used rockets were detached and left in space. The interesting thing about growing big is not only that it grows larger in size and volume, but the frontiers keep changing. Man's ability to create new scenarios is the specie's distinctive ability.

The sociologists know that in many ways what is valid in a group context is also valid in the individual context. There are no limits to group dynamics of humans, from submarines settling at the bottom of the ocean bed to rockets roaring beyond Mars. The limits have yet to be set. In a manner of speaking, much of this is true for individuals.

There is a popular quip which says, 'When one sees a difficult task, and the person doesn't feel up to it, the question to ask is not why it should be done. But the question to ask is, "why shouldn't it be done?"' Thus, it is that the deep strengths of a human being so often left untapped sprout, and his evolution from a normal mortal to an emancipated one becomes a splendid trek.

This can apply to careers, this can apply to enterprise building, and it can apply to almost anything and anywhere because in the ultimate sense, cosmic energy is boundless. Those who are created in that same image, or who believe that they have an element of the internal energy in them, obviously can't lead a bounded life.

It is this which gives the unique flavor to life which converts all trials and tribulations that life has in store into triumphs and achievements. The poet said, "I fall upon the thorns of life. I bleed." The achiever said, "The thorns of life propel me to move faster and quicker to get beyond the range which takes me to the lush grasses and the beckoning scenario, which unfolds as I keep walking towards the horizon."

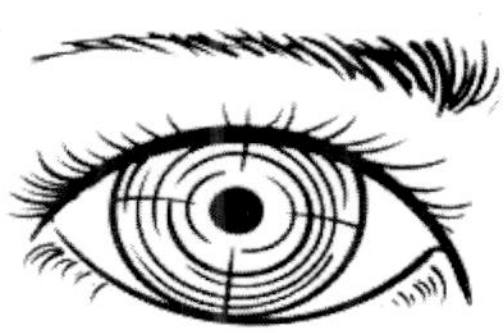

To each his own, each one sets his own limits, and therefore, enjoys his own efforts or is the victim of his own self-imposed limitations. That is the beauty of existence, and all that is around and in the universe.

Mythology and Learning

What this chapter is, also, about

The fact that mythologies exist in all societies, and moreover, are remarkably similar across distant lands, highlights the fact that they are similar to "universal truths". While the values in each society may be fine-tuned as per the life of the people in that society, almost all values are derived from mythology. Therefore, if we are to understand a culture better and to be successful in that culture, there could be few better priorities than to understand their mythologies. This is equally true to understand one's own culture, for there is no better way to appreciate one's own language and culture, than to learn about another. Therefore, one who does not pay attention to myths and cultural aspects, does so at his/ her own risk.

Sociologically speaking, it is always tricky to get a perspective on proximity. One's own experiences get interpreted through a prism of the immediate impact. This is as true of individual group experiences as it is of larger collective experiences. Sometimes, one overestimates the significance of the present, and at others, underestimates it. An illustration will make the point clearer, and place the discussion which follows in perspective. The earliest remnants of homo sapiens as they are today go back to at least 60000-70000 years. Life on this planet had existed many millennia before that. And yet, many millennia before that ˉ so long ago that it is difficult to estimate with any accuracy ˉ the present landmass of this planet as a unified entity. Gradual and almost continual shifts through tectonic movements created the present landmass geography. Of the many evidences for it, one witnesses how in parts of the geography, coastal lines of the continents spacing each other fit into each other like a jigsaw puzzle. That is another story.

Closer to the 60-70,000 date line, recorded history in very few cases goes back prior to 10,000 BC. Even if 10,000 BC be considered a watershed for convenience sake; it is difficult, if not impossible, to pin any accurate date to the remnants of Stone Age or any other Paleolithic age. There was a time when even the Stone Age looked young, and the subsequent eras which follow down to the time of pyramids seem to have only just begun history. Folk memory gradually emerged from the shadows, and no one is quite clear, how and in what form. The society evolved, as it continues to do today, and the current technological interventions figure amongst the most definitive interventions in shaping human form, history, and society.

There was a time on this planet when across continents, values and theories of society and statecraft, were by and large similar. Respect for the elders who were considered a source of knowledge, information, and learning. The current fashion of questioning, assertion, and claiming independence were not only unheard of, but unthinkable. Females were supposed to have

respect for the males, and the males fancied themselves to be of significance by adoring, admiring feminine attributes, and sometimes fashioning female symbols of preservation as the ultimate deliverer of mankind. Children were taught to be respectful to the parents who had sacrificed for them. The blessings of the parents were considered a definite variable in the prosperity of the children. People were taught to be respectful to the leaders, in many cases, the kings and the emperors. Over time, all this changed.

This cannot be the place to annotate the evolution, but the most significant changes took place arising out of two technological revolutions. The revolution of the automobile, and the revolution of the pill. Revolution of the automobile reduced the vagaries of movement from one place to the other, and especially, the females need not necessarily have to be escorted for safety. The revolution of the pill gave to the woman at a mass level a control over her body. Her risk of carrying unwanted conception was drastically reduced, and she could walk away from a physical relationship with the same kind of shrug of the shoulder which the males had always enjoyed. Such a fundamental, and if it maybe called tectonic shift, was bound to affect social structure, power structure, and indeed the roots of the social ecosystem. The result was a significant impact on social paradigms, paradigms of governance, and decision making.

Across these generational shifts, the one continuum of annotation, if it maybe so called, of folklore and mythology has remained a constant. Anchored somewhere in a remote past, so hazy and distant, that it's almost impossible to chronicle, mythology retained memories of events of which even historical evidences have been wiped out. An illustration would clarify the intent of these remarks. There is a mythology around some flood which took place in a holy past, being

transmitted through generations, in various forms, in various regions, with almost similar echoes. There is the story of Noah, *Book of Genesis* 6:5-9:17. The South Asian subcontinent remembers it through the story of Manu and the fish. The Tigris-Euphrates region around Babylon had references to it in Utnapishtim, and believe it or not, there is the flood myth of Hawaii.

The doubting Thomases can read about the flood of Kahinile-i. Subsequent scholars have researched on this area, and what is quite clear is, this planet experienced such an enormous flood sometime in the hoary past, that almost all human civilization got nearly wiped out. Of course, the Newtonian scholar, and those wedded to the altar of inquiry, which has to be evidence based will find no trace of this flood anymore. It's difficult to argue with a belief, even if the belief has to do with belief in logic and evidence. In this backdrop, it's possible to put the discussion of mythology in perspective.

The distinguishing features of mythology, and there are mythologies from all parts of the world, is largely common. All mythologies talk of some society, some connect it between individuals, some experiences, some dreams, and of course, gaps between dreams and reality. In many mythologies, plants speak and so do creatures. The almost universal personification of all beings is amazingly present. The collective memory is never questioned, and of course, there is the presence of the other world, and even the underworld. It is difficult to examine all this in a template of logical, evidence based analysis. Much of this is long before scripts existed, writing was known, and of course, the preservation of material on which one would write is still a matter of just a few centuries, which is a small portion of the life span of humans on this planet.

The deduction is simple. Mythologies have a place in collective memory, and like everything else, there are mythologies and mythologies. Sigmund Freud thought of myths as a collective projection of the processes taking place in the unconscious mind, a kind of a shared dream. Those who know Sigmund Freud know that for him, everything began with the unconscious for which of course no evidence could ever be produced. There are other views on mythology, and not all of them are abstruse to the point of incomprehension. Consider the *Hadith*. *Hadith* is to Islam, what, roughly *Talmud* is to Judaism. *Koran* and *Hadith* are two different things. *Hadith* deals with traditions attributed to Prophet Mohammed.

Max Mueller, celebrated for his sojourns which led credibility to Indian scriptures when compared to the Western ones, believed that mythology was inherent to human existence. He went to great lengths in establishing a relationship between language and thought. And a free interpretation of Max Mueller's view would tantamount to considering mythology as a penetration into the childhood of mankind. It needs to be quickly added that, that pattern of creating and nurturing that kind of memory, embellished, and fully blown up took its own course across millennia of human existence. New ones being added, old ones being modified, and whatever else takes place in a creative oasis. Homer flourished on mythology.

Thomas Mann, the Nobel prize winner of literature in 1929, took mythology as the foundation of life, where formulations exist into which "life flows when it reproduces its traits out of the unconscious". The purpose of this text cannot be a scholarly exploration of the contours of mythology, but the reason of the preceding paragraphs is simple. Whether we like it or not, we are all a part of mythology, and mythology is a part of all our thinking. Individuals who have broken out of this connect are few, and there is little evidence to prove that their logical processes

can bear the rigor of their own approach of the scientific method.

Welcome then to the world of where animals speak, plants feel, and the natural processes communicate in a language which human beings use. The interesting part of mythology, of course, has many aspects. One of them is the creation of a value system. It remains valuable even when people resist it, and tend to destroy it. This is so because mythological shadows are cast upon behavior, success, and failure. Mythologies create belief, and get etched on the collective psyche. One may not know where heaven or the underworld are, but almost all societies have stories related to them.

Perhaps this is a model which comes in handy to explain the unexplained aspects of human life ¯ where logic stops, and experience takes over, giving way to belief which often creates paradigms of solace and continuing to struggle. One is never able to fully answer the question, "struggle for what?" The Vedantist stops short of the conclusion by talking of it as the logic of *Maya*. Others talk of it as waiting for the day of deliverance. Yet, if one thing exists, it is the certainty that the coming day has to be faced just as the present one has to be lived, and one is impacted what has passed the preceding day.

That is the power of mythology in our lives, a mythology where divinity in its human incarnation has many arms with abilities to transform oneself, of human beings who could ascend to heavens like Nachiketa to find answers to a simple question which bothers us all, the question of what is beyond death? The thin line of distinction between popular oral folk tales, legends and stories is always a tricky one. It is the values which it creates which play out in most people.

There are typologies of mythologies and oral traditions. In India, the simplest stories of *Panchatantra* and *Hitopdesh* have created foundations of a sound social order, through instrumentalities which not only entertain but also enlighten. People will get meaning out of these stories, as per their worth and capability. This is a remarkably resilient method of child learning and adult learning. But the story doesn't end there.

There are parallel myths, and there are mysteries of myths. Scholars have discovered similarities in mythologies of the Jews and the North American tribes. The collective memories sometimes look amazingly similar. The scientific answers to all this is still to come, but then each generation, seeks the answer to the questions which it is faced with in the limitations of a human life span. Ordinarily, across cultures, human life span has rarely been calibrated to measure more than a hundred years. At the end of the day, a hundred years is perhaps, to use an analogy, smaller than a speck of dust on the total canvas of existence of living species as also of the humans.

In a strange way, mythologies represent an approximation of truth, and collective memory, which can lighten the path, if intelligently filtered, wisely used, and sensibly applied to everyday issues, and not such regular everyday issues too, if one is seeking answers without experimenting with oneself.

Living By One's Word

What this chapter is, also, about

In modern times, keeping one's word is considered too much of a burden, and is (often) easily excusable. However, it is precisely in such times that keeping's one's word make someone go from "average" to "exceptional", if people can be classified that way. A man can get along reasonably well without needing to be true to his word all the time; but someone who is true to his word, gains a reputation that is the envy of all and is hard to match. While the short term challenges in keeping one's word are well known, this chapter seeks to point out some of the long term benefits that are not equally well known or appreciated.

Civil society owes its survival through commitment to an unstated, but a well understood civil code. Different cultural milieu have formalized this in different manners, from the 10 commandments in the *Bible* to portions of *Hadith* to dictums found in *Upanishads* and the list can go on. These unwritten codes are extant everywhere. Clearly, in the primaeval world, say that amongst the tribes, and in large patches of the non-tribal areas, there is also no exception. Yet civil society is a must in practice to make sure that causing hurt, death, or worse to another person is something which the community in which it would be enacted would not accept, and there would clearly be a punishment backed by the understanding of the issue in the larger consciousness of the community where this act was enacted. This has to do with not just life and limb, but to gender relationships, and relationships of property and possession, not to overlook patterns of market transaction.

Exchange is fundamental to human existence because nobody can produce all of what he needs. History is a testimony of different media of exchange, barter of product for product, product for services, or services for services, and the list is endless. Attempts to standardize such exchanges have been through bullion, token currency, and now of cryptocurrency. That is a separate issue. What one seeks to focus on here is the importance of the word in all this. It's difficult to form a running set of volumes of codifications, of rules, and regulations which touch collective life.

This has not, however, made any civil society give up its continuing attempts at codification. When codification is seen to be inadequate; then there is talk of rules and regulations. When rules and regulations prove inadequate; then people refer to practices. There is a case for all this, just as there is a case to realize that, however diligently and exhaustively it be done, it would always be short of being comprehensive.

Hence, one gets back to the importance of the word (promise, pledge, or guarantee) in collective life. Anyone's word to anyone else rides the horse of credibility. It would be impossible to deal with anyone if constantly the urge was to seek documentation, evidence, and a court of appeal for punitive

action in case it is violated. Hence, the place of word in civil society is central. It is the algorithm on which every relationship, dyadic, or otherwise, would ride. Yet somehow, the value of word seems to have many levels of operations ¯ in relationships, one to one, one to many, many to many, and so on. In fact, the temptation to say one thing, and not live up to it has such a broadband of coverage that it would begin with giving someone a time to meet, and not living up to it, which travels through many experiences to promising someone something, and not delivering it.

The temptation to violate one's word comes in many forms, including the urge to optimize. Illustratively, if one gives time to someone on a given date, and something more attractive with a revenue overtone arises for attention on the same date and same time; the chances are more than even that people would forget about the preceding word given, and gravitate to the situation which has a monetary worth.

For the sake of elaboration and argument, even if that be accepted, the truth is that not all go back, as in the first case to tell the party that they can't honor their word. For many, just disappearing is a convenient option. It is deemed convenient because of a lack of sense of any responsibility to anything or anyone. It is convenient because the unstated question at the back of the mind is, if I don't deliver my word, what can he do about it? Yet, one more blow has been delivered to one of the basic pillars of human relationships, namely not leaving the other person misunderstanding of where he is with reference to you. But unfortunately in many parts of the world, this trend is growing. India is an endemic area. The writer of these lines has tried to elaborate upon this theme, in formal and informal groups, and quite candidly, a generous feedback was the writer was overdoing his concern. These things

happen, not only in India, but everywhere, "one has to learn to live with these things".

The matter may not be as simple as that, even if one were to overlook the issues of confidence, collaboration, and understanding. The issue is it hurts business, productivity, and not the least relationships. If one has a civil community, where each one is known not to have any credibility of word, then let alone dealing with another community, even within the same community, relationships are difficult to manage. If these relationships don't exist, business and the civil society will also have to pay the price.

The above statement is neither profound, nor original, but needs repeating because it has to be drummed into the psyche of morality of people. Simple matters like holding a meeting become dubious when people don't turn up or on time. Many examples can be given, but to put it simply in the interest of brevity, any collective work becomes impossible because each task to be done cannot carry a sworn affidavit.

In organization design physiology, work gets accomplished when each job situation is clear on tasks receivable, and tasks deliverable. The incumbent of that job adds value to the tasks he receives, and with that value addition passes on to the next incumbent as tasks delivered. If word is not honored, the chain gets broken. The pathetic attempts to laugh it off, or make jokes about it, or worse claim, "I am that way only" needs no comment. Forget the bad English of the explanation given. When delivered with a chuckle or nonchalance, that sentence is the trigger of much agony people inflict upon themselves as a community.

It is difficult to imagine what life would be, if each one was to determine his course of action by the immediate logic of convenience. At a higher level of existence, organized word would be impossible, civil society would be tainted, and in a more grotesque manner, even accidents would be commonplace. A universal consciousness on the value of word is needed. Of course it's possible that after giving a word, exigencies crop up. They can and do crop up; but not even communicating it cannot be eulogized with a logic, "How does it matter? These are minor things."

Nothing is minor, and nothing is major. What is minor and what is major will be determined by the person who is affected by the default. Not turning up at the altar may be minor for a partner to be; it may undo the life of the partner who turned up. These instances are neither mythical, imaginary, nor stretch imagination. The core issue is not that sometimes one's word cannot be kept. The issue is how one reacts about one not keeping one's word, or indeed, to somebody else not keeping his word. The author of these lines believes that life has been kind to him, and that's another story, but then he can do no better than to share the results of his own experiences.

In giving assignments or making appointments, the writer of these lines has followed a simple principle, a commitment once made is a commitment made. If at 12 o'clock on a given Thursday, he has given word to attend a meeting, he will do so. The person would not barter it if that person had another offer for that slot with remuneration. This has worked wonders for his branding, but caused havoc to his social acceptability. Here comes the crunch. He is taken as strange to say the least, and impossible at the worst.

Numerous people have tried to explain to this person that it doesn't work that way. Their advice need not be debated here, but the story also doesn't end there.

Even for those who are hit by a betrayal of the word ¯ one is coining a phrase for the want of a better phrase ¯ betrayal of the word is not usually seen as heinous. The average reaction is, these things happen. These things needn't be taken so seriously. How does it matter? The truth is nothing matters in life because one was dust to begin with, and to dust one returns. The choice can only be between being reduced to ashes or dust. Clearly nothing much to choose from as far as this issue is concerned. But if one is a little less philosophical, the business of keeping word is not that trivial a matter. It is the hallmark of a civil society.

The number of people who observe their word, their style and class of observing their word is an index of the kind of culture, and the level of evolution of that society. Be it business, be it governance, be it any interactive relationship, keeping one's word is the cornerstone of the edifice of any relationship. It may be sad, but it is true that in many parts of our society, whereas non-observance of the word is treated with casualness, equally observance of the word is not given the kind of recognition which it merits. It's rarely that a person is evaluated, promoted, or inducted ¯ chose your one ¯ on the dimension of his ability to keep his word. Such traits are neither publicly acknowledged, nor applauded.

Yes, every society does have people who keep their word, but this is taken as their trait, much like they have two eyes, two ears and one nose. There is no value attached to it. Rarely will a person be introduced as a person who keeps his word, or rarely will somebody be excommunicated as it were, for not keeping his word. This is not being recognized quite yet, but this hurts businesses. It hurts governance, it hurts the quality of interpersonal relationships. In case of nations which have gone beyond their territorial boundaries and savored success, keeping one's word has always been found to be somewhere a part of their value pantheon.

Life is easier when you know that the person you are dealing with is honorable, and somewhere, it is an encouragement to reciprocate that brand by being reliable in one's own word. Who knows someday, our nation would awaken to that dawn, and the fettered energies of a group of credible people dealing with each another on credibility and value of word would be able to unleash their energy as only how keeping one's word can.

What Earns a Brand?

What this chapter is, also, about

Every individual needs to be a brand, for without one, how does one capitalize on the quality delivered? The only question then is, how important is it to have one? This chapter sets out to answer that question. For any professional who aspires to rise to the top of their field, building a brand, and continually investing in it to keep it relevant, is possibly one of the most important (and least understood) tasks. Hopefully, after reading this chapter, the reader would be better prepared to ask the right questions while setting out on his/ her journey.

There are people who don't understand cricket, but they know of Lords. They also know that for many cricketers playing at the Lords is the realization of a dream. And if cricket is to be watched, it better be watched at Lords, rather than on the grounds of Sydney. The two cricket grounds have something in common, and that's of course, cricket.

Those who know about cricket grounds know that a cricket ground has a substantial part of its pavilion infrastructure, like a mini-city, with its bath, jacuzzies, workouts *et al* meant to tone the body of the people who go undergo stamina test through hours of grueling conditions on the greens. Yes, the old renews itself, and the writer himself in a technology institute has had a desktop from the days of the mainframe that is 1983-84. It struck him while dealing with 286 to how wires were relayed and points were fixed, unhinged, re-fixed, layouts changed as the system graduated from 286 to 386 to 486 to Pentium I, Pentium II, Pentium III, Pentium IV, all in a period of less than 20 years.

The story of technological change which is neither unique, nor exclusive to this engineering institution. He always found himself blessed because the institute would take care of the upgradation of the hardware, and would appropriately, after the initial two or three years, also provide the software and the maintenance infrastructure. So be it. This narrative is not a standalone description of how technological and some hardware upgradation requires wiring, re-wiring, junctions, energy sockets, and a whole infrastructure of delivery of which even a lot of the computer scientists are happily unaware, let alone have the knowledge to handle.

The Sydney stadium was constructed much after Lords, and today is a showpiece of modern updated technological amenities, which many first class cricket players have used, and aspire to use.

All this does not surface in the columns of cricket commentators, nor indeed, in the narratives on the screen which display records, and shots from the heritage collection. But this indeed is the backbone of first class cricket on a ground where first class cricket is played. The

Lords also has an infrastructure which is pretty avant garde. Irrespective of the good job done, the high finesse of the ground, and its infrastructure does reveal itself to the discriminating eye the technological journey of updation. Irrespective of all this, Lords remains Lords, and nobody would swap a match on the Sydney ground for a match in the Lords.

That's a brand name. Indeed, that's the brand. It is an encapsulation of a visualization, of a dream situation fed, garnished, and whipped up with legends, stories, and imaginative projections of what it would have been to see a player of legendary proportions walking out of the Lords pavilion to take the crease. It is a mix of reality and imagination taking wings, which is also something which feeds a brand. There are other feeders to a brand. Class is one. Cambridge remains Cambridge, irrespective of the fact that say the coming of a modern discipline like management was one of the later entries to the Cambridge curriculum. For years it was stuck in Churchill college.

Disciplines like history and their ilk have been long in the Cambridge curriculum, or that of Oxford, and people still go to that university to pick up a masters, say, in a discipline like history of technology, whose job prospects are not exactly the best as compared to what the compensation for a systems analyst would be. Put simply, be it cricket or educational institutions, brands as an entity have their own lifecycle. The story doesn't end there. The amazing thing is brands change. There was a time, not so very long ago in India, where anything Japanese was supposed to be cheap, low technology, and therefore, to be derided. This was soon after the Second World War. Those readers who were around in the early 50s, and saw Raj Kapoor's *Shriman 420* would remember the popular song, *"Mera Joota hai Japani, Yeh patloon Inglistani..."* The shot had Raj Kapoor putting up his right leg, and then

his left leg, to show a gaping hole in his old shoes. The pantaloon which he wore was a caricature of Charlie Chaplin suit. Other detailing may not be necessary. The lilting music of this song survived over half a century, and people forgot what *Japani* stood for. Now, to the new generation, *Joota hai Japani* (my shoes are Japanese) means little other than that I have foreign shoes. Not only the brand, but the meaning has undergone transformation. That is also what happens to a brand. Popular image imbues to it a character which transforms over time.

There was a time in the Indian educational system where going to Presidency college was a status symbol. Patna College, founded in 1863, was a hotbed of scholars from history to languages, and much else. A degree from Patna College was magical. From about late 60s, the transformation began, and forget Presidency, Patna, or Allahabad University, even the destinations changed. And the buzzwords were Harvard, Yale, Princeton, and the list is too well known to be reiterated. The amusing thing is that American scholar's field tickled by this brand projection in some of the third world countries like India. Harvard is not considered the first amongst universities in America always. There are years where it has been ranked 4th or lower in the hierarchy, and there are other universities which have a better rating than Harvard. Yet in India, the opening gambit of a conversation, or a speech has few statements which have a better gambit of success than saying, "When I was in Harvard...".

The force of a brand name is such that people will deliberately get duped to display their status by flashing a brand which has

caught people's imagination. A Rolex watch is typical. In some of the beaches of South East Asia holiday destinations, a Rolex watch can be bought for US $8. Believe it or not, it works. The question is only for how long, and with what accuracy. But in the cocktail circuit, nobody has the time to ask the time. But everyone has the time to look at the apparel, and where ladies are concerned, the brand of the handbag; where men are concerned, the brand of the watch. In case it is not noticed, the conversation is steered to have a reference to this, and the doubting Thomases can try it to see that it does actually affect the response.

That's the magic of a brand in its myriad shapes and colors. The story doesn't end there. Brands have an aura, a lifecycle, and affect not only products, but also relationships. There are cases of Indian mothers in law or fathers in law selecting a daughter in law, or a son in law because of the brand of the family name. If there has been an Advocate General in the family; a couple of vice chancellors; a set of people who have arrived politically; or businessmen who stay on a mall road of a hill station, have four or five shops; then that daughter in law or son in law is a much more prized "catch". The way alliances take place in a substantial section of the Indian marriage market is a tell-tale story of brand playing a role.

The trouble with the foregoing description is that to the best of the information of the writer of these lines, no serious study of this kind of a profile process has been subjected to a scholastic analysis to understand the underpinnings. Perhaps the proximity of the process to everyday life is daunting. Irrespective of that, the need remains, and like any need will get addressed someday. Somebody did say that nature abhors vacuum.

What is much oftener the subject matter of scholastic analysis is the effort which is put in in the advertising segment of the marketing component of the management area. There are dedicated groups working on how a brand is created, and media is one of the vehicles through which this is attempted. The media tries visuals, graphics, repetition, and riding

piggyback on celebrities to create a brand. The glib assumption that quality pays off is a half-truth. Quality to pay off must have a brand. To have a brand, one must attract. To attract, one must evoke the visualization in the respondent's mind, and that visualization would be embedded in empathy.

The process is complex, and has the obligation to meet the aspirations of not only the new entrants of business, but keep lubricating the growth needs of the established ones. This cannot be a place for a research analysis of how brand building is breaking ground, and how it impacts everything, from marketing campaigns to political image building. There are some competent people looking at these issues. What every aspiring celebrity needs is to have cheerleaders.

Shakespeare may have opined in one of his plays through one of his characters, "Repetition? What is there in a repetition? Often got without deserving, and lost without reason." Much wisdom is attributed to Shakespeare, not the least because of his ability to play with words. Some of these claims are never established, because the person who forwards these claims is unable to recall the play, the act, the scene, the character, and the line where this statement exists. That doesn't matter. But Shakespeare is a brand. It has been so for over a century, and it gives status to a wise reworded statement if it's credited to Shakespeare. That is also how a brand is created. The brand of Shakespeare itself was created by the critique of Shakespearean writing by the commentator named Bradley. Not many people outside the narrow confines of those who have done a specialized course of Shakespeare have heard of Bradley. It doesn't matter.

Brand is an impact, and it evokes a response. If the effect is created, the means are seldom subjected to the scrutiny of authenticity and reliability. Put simply, brand is plays with visualization and imagery ¯ the encapsulation of a dream and ideal. It's an aspirational vehicle. People love to ride their aspirations. As Voltaire said, "If there isn't a God, we would have to create one." Similarly, if the word brand did not exist with the aura which it has to get the effect it causes; one would have had to create the process to gain fulfilment to that desirable goal of attributes.

Does The Winner Take All?

What this chapter is, also, about

As we come to the close of this book, it is only fit that we explore the common misunderstanding around winning, and what it takes to be a winner in the long term. History is replete with examples of leaders who have been fooled by the statement, "Winner takes all", and who went on to lose it all soon thereafter. It is hoped that this chapter provides some insights into what to do once you have won, and how to truly "win it all". Wishing you all the very best in your journey called life!

The homo sapiens at a certain stage of his evolution found life too complex a process to understand. It found the chores of contending with nature and each other far too complex for unmitigated enjoyment. So he devised several escape vehicles. One of them was literature. He would write poems, where the feminine character always symbolized gentility, beauty, kindness, often not receiving sympathy, but above all, elegance and aesthetic excellence. The male poet would pine after it, would get rejected, would persist, and a whole psycho-drama was generated. (Those were the happy days where gender equity hadn't destroyed foundations of emotion, where women were given the image of being almost beyond the world.)

Similarly, the homo sapiens found too many complexities to contend with. So proverbs arose. The defining characteristic of a proverb is nobody bothers to test it. Everyone wants to use it. Every use adds a few millimeters to the heels. Hence, the plethora of proverbs. Entire books have been published containing proverbs. This cannot be a place for even a brief enumeration. But not to enumerate any could lead to confusion. Hence, let's take the proverb, "All is fair in love and war". Or, "Fortune smiles on the brave". Or, even the simpler one, "The winner takes all".

These have never been subjected to a deep scholastic analysis, or indeed, a scientific scrutiny. Whoever said a belief needs scrutiny? In fact, if you question somebody's belief, say in a religious or spiritual matter, you are not sufficiently a cultured to know that beliefs cannot be questioned. It is another matter that beliefs of armourily evolved communities and people are more sacrosanct than beliefs of people who are not so armourily evolved. Hence, the beliefs of tribals can be sneered at, but equally preposterous beliefs of the technologically evolved societies must be respectfully referred to, and on no occasion be ever subjected to scrutiny. The claim is laid that technology has facilitated the movement of this planet towards a more egalitarian order. The truth is technology has widened and deepened the rift with whatever semblance of egalitarian order the world ever had. Nevertheless, the myth is technology is a great leveler. Another proverb.

In the case of this proverb, namely technology is a great leveler. It owes its success, and a phenomenal one at that, because of the half-truths which it carries. Something often becomes a proverb because it captures a limited truth. Consider the statement, there is freedom for the brave. Of course, there is freedom for the brave. No one, however, talks of the number of brave people who lost lives seeking freedom. It really boils down to what captures the imagination of which color.

Hence, the winner takes all. This statement has been used, abused, thrown around, and is considered the raison d'etre for the powerful of the moment, and the logic for having things their way. They have never read Fay's *The History of World War I*, who gloriously describes how the French minister at the concluding Versailles conference scored immense gains for the French cause by raising embarrassing questions to groups feeling awkward at the wrong times. Versailles settlement was not the most-fair settlement ever in human history. But it would have been far worse if the winners had indeed taken all.

The proposition is simple, any activity, or negotiation has several modular components. The result of activity in any modular component is determined not only by a set of exogenous forces, but who is the smarter and the more deeply thinking person in the group at work. The winner taking all is a simplified algorithm, which eliminates insight into the nature of human dynamics, and discourages any growth to a higher level of sensitivity and maneuver. Nevertheless, winner taking all is also a subset of what is at stake. Say in wooing, the case is clear. The winner does take all. The boy or the girl who wins against the competition would have the partner to marry presumably for keeps.

In case of physical occupation of a territory, the boardroom of a corporate, or indeed the possession of an asset, the winner does take all. There are no half way houses. There cannot be. Hence, if it's plausible to argue that like both statements, the response to the statement "Winner takes all" is sometimes yes, sometimes no, and sometimes the smarter one gets some strategic advantages, and would also have to strategically lose some advantages.

Indeed, this is what life is about. You win some, you lose some, and you negotiate the others. Winner takes all is a great simulant for effort, branding, making a point, and gaining the first right of refusal. These are not inconsiderable advantages. And, if the label is the winner taking all, so be it. It is equally true that if you want to keep what you seek to aspire for after winning; it is best to be generous while winning, but judiciously so. The strategic interests cannot be mortgaged. That's where diplomacy is needed.

At the same time, if the adversary is not propitiated, he would live to fight another day. In all things a judgement to concede what may not be critical for keeping, to establish a relationship with the so called vanquished is a must. It is necessary to realize that no battle is a terminal one. Therefore, no winning can be the final one.

One proverb deserves another. There is a statement, "He who fights and runs away, lives to fight another day." The winner can take all, but then that all may not be worth keeping without ease of mind. In the ultimate analysis, who takes what is also a factor of who can keep what? Hence, there is a larger wisdom of behavior, and a larger wisdom of the art of the possible.

It's true proverbs are formulations of years of experimentation, empiricism, and wisdom. Yet by definition, this is a continuing process. There can't be any definitive posturing on this. Consider the following: "Look before you leap", but "He who hesitates is lost". There are others, "Two heads are better than one", but "Too many cooks spoil the broth."

The key is judgement. The absolute rules are seldom absolute. Hence, to the question, "Does the winner take all?" there is no substitute but to say, "Exercise your judgement". Decide whether a person could take all, and if so, could he keep it all? Or is it better to share and negotiate for a settlement which may be more enduring, for who knows, what one kept as the booty of winning may turn out to be a liability in the long run?